The Journey to NexGen Island

A Fable of Growth, Collaboration, and Leadership

Stephen C. Kincaid

BrainPower Bytes

For all the dreamers, the doers, and the difference-makers, who, through this book, dare to believe in the power of personal transformation. May your thirst for knowledge and your pursuit of growth become the beacon that inspires others to strive for more. This journey is dedicated to you, for in your desire to be more and do more, you hold the power to change the world.

Contents

Introduction

Welcome to an extraordinary journey—a journey not across geographical terrains but the vast landscape of your own potential. "The Journey to NexGen Island" is not merely a book, but a catalyst designed to ignite transformation within you and equip you with the mindset tools needed for effective leadership and personal growth.

My name is Stephen C. Kincaid, and through my initiative Brain-Power Bytes, I am committed to inspiring and empowering the next generation of leaders. Having navigated my own share of life's ups and downs, I recognize the critical role that mindsets play in overcoming adversity, seizing opportunities, and driving growth.

This book unfolds the intriguing story of Alexander, who, like many of us, finds himself yearning for change in a world that seems stagnant. Guided by the insightful Sage, Alexander embarks on a quest to NexGen Island—a place filled with challenges that are symbolic of the key mindsets that drive success and growth.

But this isn't just Alexander's journey—it's yours too. The book is divided into two parts for this reason. The first part tells the story of Alexander's expedition and his encounters with the ten mindsets on NexGen Island. You'll find yourself walking in Alexander's shoes, facing and overcoming challenges that test your resilience, adaptability, and will to grow.

In the second part, we delve deeper. We explore each mindset in greater detail, providing insights, tips, and strategies to help you incorporate these principles into your own life. It's your personal playbook—a guide to unlock your potential and transform your perspective.

Whether you're a young professional beginning your career, a seasoned veteran seeking to amplify your impact, or an aspiring leader aiming to drive change, this book is your compass. It's an invitation to look beyond the ordinary, to recognize that growth isn't a destination—it's an ongoing journey.

So, let's embark on this extraordinary voyage together. Let's explore the mindsets that can catapult us to new heights of success and fulfillment. Your journey to NexGen Island awaits. Are you ready to set sail?

Preface

In the seemingly uneventful town of Stagnant Shores, wedged between a monotonous bay and an ever-grey sky, dwelled our hero, Alexander. The town's character was as static as its name suggested, its brick-and-mortar buildings echoing the unchanging rhythm of its inhabitants' lives.

Amid the ceaseless clatter of the town's factory, a tune as common to Alexander's ears as his own heartbeat, stirred a yearning for something beyond the routine. Alexander's daily life was woven with the threads of monotony, from his predawn chores to his relentless work at the assembly line. But within him, a spark of curiosity flickered, a spark that refused to be extinguished by the dampness of his surroundings.

Every day, Alexander would escape the din of machinery and retreat to the factory rooftop. Sitting atop the world he knew, his gaze would wander to the horizon, aching for the world he didn't. His heart echoed with the stories Sage, a wise elderly woman, shared of lands where the spirit of innovation roared like a fierce wind, where the quest for knowledge was the anchor that held communities together.

In the reflective hush of the night, Alexander found himself torn between the comfort of the familiar and the allure of the unknown. The tales of NexGen Island felt like a distant dream, a fascinating tale that both excited and unnerved him. Could there exist a land so different from his own, a place where growth wasn't merely a dream but a way of life?

The decision to embark on a journey towards the unknown was one that Alexander wrestled with for countless nights. His heart battled between the security of what he knew and the promise of what he didn't. Amid murmurs of concern and whispers of fear, Alexander made a choice. A choice that was as much about him as it was about the future of Stagnant Shores.

And so, under the break of dawn, Alexander found himself at the edge of a decision as vast as the sea before him. As he stepped into a modest boat, the first chapter of his adventure began to unfurl. The comforting silhouette of his town started to fade, replaced by the boundless sea and the promise of NexGen Island. His heart throbbed in his chest, a dance of fear, anticipation, and raw excitement. The echo of Stagnant Shores was now behind him; ahead lay the symphony of the unknown.

From the comfortable predictability of his life, Alexander had chosen the thrill of uncertainty, the adventure of the undiscovered. His journey was more than a voyage across the sea; it was a leap towards a different future, a future ignited by the promise of NexGen Island.

With every paddle stroke, the winds whispered tales of the trials that lay ahead, of challenges as unpredictable as the sea itself, of an island where learning never ceased, and innovation was a way of life. Alexander could only guess what lay in store for him, but he knew one thing for certain - his life was about to change in ways he couldn't begin to imagine.

And so, our tale begins, a tale of one man's courage and his pursuit of growth. This is Alexander's "Journey to NexGen Island". As we unfurl this story, we invite you to sail alongside Alexander, to ride the waves of uncertainty with him, and to explore the potential of NexGen Island.

The voyage has just begun.

Chapter 1
The Voyage Begins

The faint light of dawn gently caressed the sleepy facade of Stagnant Shores, coaxing the town and its inhabitants from their slumber. Life stirred in a predictable rhythm, the quiet simplicity of their world as constant as the ebb and flow of the nearby sea.

In the heart of this tranquil rhythm, a dissonance resonated, personified in a single man - Alexander. His existence, like a vibrant splash of color against the monotone canvas of Stagnant Shores, was punctuated with a restless thirst for knowledge, a ceaseless quest for growth.

Every day, as the sun journeyed across the sky, Alexander moved through the unvarying pattern of his life. His daily work at the town's factory was a choreographed dance of routine, the same dance performed by everyone in Stagnant Shores. But where others found comfort in this dance, Alexander found only restlessness.

His heart was stirred not by the monotony of everyday tasks but by the tantalizing lure of the world beyond. He often found himself gazing into the distance, his mind buzzing with questions unanswered, dreams unfulfilled. "Why should we be content with merely existing when we can live, truly live?" He would often wonder aloud.

His childhood friend, Ethan, struggling to comprehend Alexander's perspective, would simply shake his head and reply, "Alex, life here isn't bad. It's peaceful, it's secure. Isn't that enough?"

Alexander, his gaze fixed at the horizon, would smile gently. "Peaceful, yes. Secure, indeed. But enough? No, Ethan. We're capable of so much more. There's a whole world out there waiting to be discovered."

His beacon of hope amidst this sea of conformity was Sage, the elderly recluse residing at the town's fringe. Sage was a bridge to the world outside, her tales a spark to Alexander's dreams. Her stories of NexGen Island, a place humming with innovation and continuous growth, resonated deeply with his desire for change.

Alexander knew then, with a certainty as steady as the rising sun, that he was destined for more than the simple life of Stagnant Shores. His heart yearned for the vibrant energy of NexGen Island, the prospect of an existence fueled by continuous learning, growth, and innovation.

And so, beneath the vast canvas of the starlit sky, a vow echoed in the silence. "I will seek NexGen Island. I will bring the spirit of curiosity, of learning, back to Stagnant Shores." With this promise reverberating in his heart, Alexander readied himself for the journey of a lifetime. Little did he know then, the adventure that awaited him was unlike any tale he'd heard from Sage. It was an adventure destined to transform not only his life but also the lives of those he was leaving behind.

***

As the golden orb of sun rose higher, bathing Stagnant Shores in its morning radiance, a day of unusual bustle unfolded in the otherwise tranquil town. A whisper of change threaded its way through the town's narrow alleyways, echoing against the worn-out walls of the factory, bouncing off the salt-encrusted dockyards. At the heart of this whirlwind of activity stood Alexander, a picture of grim determination etched on his weathered face.

His peers looked on, bemusement lining their faces as they watched him move about with a sense of purpose they couldn't comprehend. Alexander packed his belongings with methodical precision - dried food, a water flask, a small knife for protection, and a notebook to chronicle his upcoming journey.

News of his impending departure spread like wildfire, the town buzzing with incredulous whispers. Amid the sea of familiar faces, Alexander's eyes sought one in particular - Ethan. His childhood friend, clad in his usual factory garb, pushed his way through the gathering, a small package clutched in his hands.

"No way you're going without these, Alex," Ethan handed him the package, a mix of concern and disbelief in his voice. "Some extra rations, a compass... Just a few things to keep you safe."

Alexander accepted the package, the reality of his journey dawning on him. His hands trembled slightly, a visible sign of the internal storm of emotions brewing within him. As he looked at Ethan, the factory loomed in the background, a stark symbol of the life he was leaving behind.

As the day aged into the evening, Alexander found himself back at the factory once more, sitting on the edge atop the roof with Ethan. The rusted metal under them creaked with years of wear, and the ocean sprawled before them, a vast expanse of endless blue. This place, their secret retreat from the world, had witnessed their dreams and shared their silence. Today, it was a witness to their farewell.

"Look at it, Ethan," Alexander gestured towards the ocean, his voice barely above a whisper, "There's a whole world beyond that horizon, a world we don't know, a world waiting to be discovered."

Ethan, his gaze following Alexander's, nodded slowly. "But why leave everything behind, Alex? This is our home."

Turning to face his friend, Alexander responded, his voice laced with conviction, "And that's why, Ethan. Because this is home. I can't bear to watch us live a life of unexplored potential. I want to bring back something better, for you, for everyone."

The sun began to set, casting long shadows across Stagnant Shores. In the dwindling light, Alexander's resolve shone bright. He was not just leaving his home; he was setting off on a quest for a better future. This was not an ending, but a beginning - the start of an extraordinary journey that would change the course of his life and the lives of those he was leaving behind.

***

A veil of night had descended upon Stagnant Shores, the gentle hum of evening tide forming a soothing lullaby. Amid this tranquil backdrop, Alexander found himself seeking the guidance of his trusted mentor, Sage. Her modest abode on the outskirts of the town felt like a safe haven where he could voice his deepest fears and doubts.

"Sage," he began, his voice barely above a whisper, "I'm afraid. Afraid of leaving the familiar behind, of what lies beyond our shores, and most of all, afraid of failing."

The wise woman, her eyes reflecting the flicker of candlelight, studied him silently. Then she nodded, her voice as calm as the still night, "Fear, Alexander, is a companion of every great journey. But remember, it is only a companion, not the master. Your fear speaks of your humility, your understanding of the magnitude of your voyage. But don't let it overshadow your courage."

Alexander listened, his mentor's words seeping into his consciousness, soothing his frayed nerves. But the tendrils of doubt still clung, wrapping around his resolve, "But what if I'm not enough? What if I can't bring about the change we hope for?"

Sage reached across, her aged hands enveloping his, "Alexander, remember this: it is those who dare to question 'what if' that make the impossible possible. The spirit of curiosity, of learning, resides within you. Trust it. Harness it. It will guide you through the darkest storms towards the horizon of enlightenment."

Her words reverberated through the silence, touching the part of him that yearned for growth, for change. The part of him that dreamt of a future where Stagnant Shores thrived with curiosity and progress. He could see it – a vision of his town no longer stagnant but alive with the spirit of NexGen Island. He could be the beacon to guide them there.

"Yes," Alexander nodded, a new determination in his gaze, "Yes, I can. For Stagnant Shores. For myself. We deserve more than just existence. We deserve growth."

With that vow made under the watchful stars, Alexander bid Sage goodbye, carrying with him her wisdom and faith. As he walked towards his humble abode, his mind wrestled with the enormity of the journey ahead. He felt fear, yes, but it was no longer a paralyzing force. It was a reminder of his responsibility, his promise. As the first ray of dawn broke over Stagnant Shores, Alexander knew in his heart that he was ready to embark on the journey to NexGen Island. He was ready to evolve, ready to ignite change, ready to be the beacon his town needed.

***

At last, the moment had arrived. As the morning sun painted a golden path across the sea, Alexander stood on the precipice of his new reality. The rhythmic roar of the sea and the whispering wind were his only companions now. His humble boat, stocked with essential supplies, seemed to share his anticipation, swaying gently in the shallows, ready to carry him to his destiny.

The taste of the salty sea air was an electrifying reminder of the journey that lay ahead. A flicker of fear stirred within him as he surveyed the vastness of the ocean, its restless waves standing between him and NexGen Island. Yet, overshadowing his fear was a blazing determination. With Sage's wisdom as his compass and the promise of a better future propelling him, he felt an undeniable pull towards the unknown.

Gritting his teeth, Alexander heaved the boat into the inviting arms of the sea. The water lapped at its hull, and the boat bobbed into motion, responding eagerly to the call of the journey. It was then that the enormity of his voyage truly hit him. Every ripple in the water, every gust of wind, carried the potential for peril or triumph. This was a journey not only across the vast ocean but into the heart of his fears, his hopes, his potential.

As Stagnant Shores dissolved into a blur, Alexander set his sight on the horizon, where the morning sun had etched a path of gold. He held the course, guiding the boat with newfound resolve. As the land disappeared, replaced by the endless expanse of the sea, he made his silent vow to the waves. "I shall return. Not as the man I was, but as the leader I aspire to be."

Under the watchful eye of the sun, Alexander, the beacon of Stagnant Shores, embarked on his odyssey towards NexGen Island. He left behind the known, steering into the enigma of the unknown, fuelled by the promise of transformation and growth. His voyage had truly begun.

***

A few hours into the voyage, as the shores of his hometown disappeared from sight, Alexander reached into his bag and found a small, worn-out book. Unfamiliar with it, he opened the cover and recognized Sage's neat handwriting on the first page, "For Alexander, to guide you when the seas get rough."

Intrigued, he turned the pages to find an assortment of maps, navigational tips, and seafaring lore, interspersed with Sage's words of wisdom. The book seemed to be a compendium of knowledge for his journey. As he began to read, Alexander felt as though Sage was right there with him, her warm voice echoing in his ears.

In one section, Sage wrote: "Alexander, the sea is like life, unpredictable and constantly changing. You cannot control the waves, but you can learn to sail your ship. Remember, the smooth sea never made a skilled sailor. It's in the storms that we grow stronger."

The words stirred something within Alexander. He paused, letting the wisdom seep in. He felt a chill run down his spine as the truth in Sage's words resonated within him. He realized that the journey ahead was not just about reaching NexGen Island, but also about embracing the trials and challenges along the way.

He mused over the pages, soaking in Sage's advice. Despite the vast, intimidating ocean around him, Alexander felt a flicker of warmth, a sense of comfort. He wasn't alone. Sage's wisdom, her teachings, were with him, guiding him just as they always had.

Gratitude welled up within Alexander as he clutched the book tighter, a priceless gift from his mentor. He gazed out at the sea, the setting sun casting a golden sheen on the horizon. His heart brimmed with resolve.

With a renewed spirit, Alexander said softly to the open sea, "I'm ready for your lessons, whatever they may be."

***

As the days rolled by, Alexander found himself alone with the sea, the sun, and his thoughts. The first few days were novel, filled with the excitement of the journey and the peace of solitude. He reveled in the simple tasks of navigation, fishing for his supper, and documenting his experiences in his journal. He relished the sight of the sunsets, each more beautiful than the last, and the sight of the stars, unimpeded by any man-made light.

But as the voyage continued, the vastness of the sea became more apparent, and the enormity of his journey started to sink in. There were moments when the solitude became too heavy, the silence too loud. At times, the sea seemed too vast, his destination too far.

One evening, as Alexander sat on the deck of his boat, staring into the endless horizon, he whispered to himself, "Did I underestimate this journey?"

Just then, a gentle gust of wind fluttered the pages of Sage's book which lay open next to him. His eyes fell on a passage, "When the journey seems too long, look at how far you've come, not how far you have to go."

The words, as if sensing his dilemma, lent him comfort. Alexander took a deep breath, feeling the salty air fill his lungs. He looked back towards the direction from where he had come, the land far out of sight. He realized he had indeed come a long way.

With a renewed sense of purpose, Alexander spent the following days not just surviving but embracing life at sea. He began to observe the sea's rhythm, the way it swelled in the morning and calmed at night. He marveled at the sight of dolphins frolicking in the distance and birds soaring high in the sky.

Yes, the journey was challenging, but Alexander was learning, growing with each passing day. He felt his fear and apprehension slowly giving way to respect and understanding, not just for the sea but for the journey itself.

The open sea, he realized, was a mirror reflecting his inner self. It was here, amidst the waves and under the open sky, that Alexander was truly beginning to understand what Sage meant when she said that the journey was more than just the distance between Stagnant Shores and NexGen Island.

***

As Alexander steadied himself, his eyes fixated on the vastness of the ocean, the magnitude of his journey started to truly dawn on him once more. The last few days at sea were eerily peaceful, filled with the calming sounds of the waves, the gentle caress of the sea breeze, and the simplicity of life away from the daily monotony of Stagnant Shores. But the seas were as unpredictable as they were vast.

Alexander was beginning to learn that. The calm sea suddenly turned restless as the clouds began to gather, turning the once clear sky into a canvas of dark hues. The change was both fascinating and frightening. His heart pounded as he noticed a wall of rain approaching him from the distance. A storm was brewing on the horizon.

In the distance, as the storm began to form, Alexander spotted something unusual. It was a flock of seagulls, circling an area in the water. Alexander had heard stories from Sage about seagulls circling waters that held mysteries beneath.

The sight filled him with a strange mix of fear and anticipation. What did the seagulls hint at? Was it just the storm they were reacting to, or was there something beneath the waters? He could not ignore the odd sensation stirring in his gut.

While his mind raced with thoughts, Alexander knew he had to prepare for the storm first. His grip tightened around the helm, his eyes set firm on the horizon, watching the approaching storm. He knew that this was only the beginning. There were countless challenges and experiences that lay ahead on his journey to NexGen Island.

As the first raindrop hit the deck of the boat, a new resolve formed in Alexander's heart. The storm was a symbol of the challenges he was ready to face, a test of his resilience, his adaptability, and his will to reach NexGen Island.

As the fury of the storm surrendered to a serene twilight, Alexander found himself cradled in a world ablaze with ethereal hues of pink and purple. His heartbeat, still marching to the drum of the tempest, began to ease. As he stabilized his craft, his gaze was drawn to the horizon, where a spectacle unlike any he had ever witnessed was unfolding.

The sea, previously a roiling beast, was now a radiant canvas. Swirling beneath the glassy surface were countless streams of shimmering light, each a river of radiant knowledge. They were streams of stories, the pulses of podcasts, and the vibrant veins of various courses, intertwined in an intricate dance of wisdom. This was the Sea of Lifelong Learning, a manifestation far beyond what Alexander had conceived.

He felt a tidal wave of reverence sweeping over him. This was a place where knowledge flowed like water, where each glowing stream offered a new route to wisdom. He was about to navigate a sea that held the collective learning of the world, a daunting yet thrilling prospect.

Reflecting on Sage's wisdom, Alexander's grip tightened around the letter, her advice echoing like a sacred mantra, "In adversity, seek wisdom. In confusion, seek understanding." He felt an incredible surge of gratitude for his mentor. Her wisdom was his beacon, guiding him even miles away from home.

Yet, as he steered his boat towards the incandescent currents, doubt shadowed his excitement. The Sea was bewitching but intimidating, its promise of knowledge vast and somewhat overwhelming. He questioned aloud, "Am I ready for this?"

His words lingered in the air before the answer surged from deep within, a roar of determination that seemed to resonate with the pulsating sea, "I am ready."

With Sage's letter clutched tightly in his hand and his resolve blazing fiercely, he directed his vessel towards the vibrant dance of knowledge. The air was thick with anticipation, the journey ahead shrouded in mystery, yet Alexander was prepared to face whatever the sea had in store for him.

However, as his boat ventured deeper into the radiant heart of the Sea of Lifelong Learning, an unexpected glimmer in the depths caught his eye. It was something concealed, something different that broke the hypnotic dance of the knowledge streams. An unfamiliar pulse that seemed to tug at his curiosity, a new enigma in this already bewildering journey.

Chapter 2
The Sea
of Lifelong
Learning

As dawn broke on the fifth day of his journey, Alexander awoke to a sight that took his breath away. The once tranquil sea had transformed into a vast expanse of shimmering waters, seemingly endless, glittering under the early rays of the sun. It was as if the very ocean had been imbued with an ethereal radiance.

At first, Alexander was taken aback. He rubbed his eyes, thinking it to be a trick of light or a result of his exhaustion. But as he continued to gaze, his eyes widened in disbelief. The surface of the sea was not just water; it was a sprawling tapestry of written words, sounds, and images. Books floated like lily pads, their pages fluttering in the gentle sea breeze. Whispered words echoed from the depths, forming a symphony of knowledge. The water itself pulsed with vibrant colors, each wave carrying a different image, an insight into a world unknown.

Alexander, initially rooted to his spot, felt a mix of emotions welling within him. Awe for the breathtaking spectacle before him, fear for the sheer enormity of the knowledge the sea represented, and an underlying thrill for what lay ahead. A soft gasp escaped his lips, "The Sea of Lifelong Learning..."

He looked at the compass in his hand, its needle unwavering in the direction of the mesmerizing sight. The journey Sage had spoken of, the first challenge of his voyage, was right there before his eyes. Alexander took a deep breath, bracing himself for the voyage through the vast sea of knowledge.

No sooner had Alexander spoken, the compass in his hand began to pulsate with a soft light, and Sage's voice filled the air around him. The voice seemed to be coming from the compass itself, a guiding echo in the silence of the sea.

"Alexander," Sage's voice resonated, both comforting and commanding, "What you see before you is not an illusion. It's the manifestation of the first stepping stone towards NexGen Island - The Sea of Lifelong Learning."

Alexander, startled by the sudden appearance of Sage's voice, clutched the compass tighter. He looked out towards the glimmering sea, as Sage continued.

"This sea symbolizes an essential part of the journey to NexGen Island and indeed, to personal growth. It stands for the wisdom of the world, an endless resource of knowledge collected and shared by thinkers, innovators, and pioneers across generations."

There was a pause as if Sage was giving Alexander a moment to let the words sink in. He stayed silent, his gaze fixated on the mesmerizing panorama of the sea. Then Sage's voice echoed once again.

"The books, the sounds, the images, they all represent different forms of learning – written wisdom, oral tradition, visual insights. This sea, Alexander, it is a reminder that learning comes in many forms and from many sources."

The voice softened, "Navigating this sea is crucial because it teaches the importance of continuous learning. To progress, to innovate, one must be open to absorbing knowledge, adapting to new information, and never ceasing to learn. To reach NexGen Island, you must learn to navigate the sea of knowledge, to embrace the wisdom it offers, and to overcome the fear of the vastness of unknown information."

As Sage's voice faded, Alexander stood contemplating her words, his gaze lingering on the shimmering horizon. His hand tightened around the compass, a newfound determination building within him. He knew this sea was a challenge he needed to overcome, a test he needed to pass. But more than anything, it was a journey he was excited to embark on - a voyage through the sea of knowledge and continuous learning.

As the boat glided into the luminous Sea of Lifelong Learning, Alexander couldn't help but feel a sense of trepidation creep in. The shimmering books, vibrant podcasts, and radiant courses surrounded him, each a beacon of knowledge in itself, illuminating the sea in a spectacle of light and color.

At first, he was overwhelmed. The enormity of it all, the endlessness of the sea was daunting. Where should he start? Which book to pick first? Which podcast to listen to? The questions raced through his mind, each vying for his attention.

He decided to start with a book, reaching out for a floating tome titled 'The Art of Innovation'. As his fingers brushed against the cover, the book burst into a stream of light, transforming into a myriad of glowing words that swirled around him. The words, heavy with wisdom and insights, swam around Alexander, their glow intensifying as they sought to impart their knowledge.

Alexander tried to grasp them, to understand, but it was like trying to catch smoke with bare hands. The words slipped from his grasp, their glow dimming as they slipped back into the sea. A sense of frustration welled up in Alexander. He was here in the Sea of Lifelong Learning, surrounded by infinite knowledge, yet he couldn't seem to grasp anything.

A podcast, in the form of a vibrant sound wave, drifted towards him next. He tried to tune in, hoping to find some insight, some wisdom to guide him. But the sound wave transformed into a cacophony of voices, each narrating a different story, a different lesson. The multitude of voices, instead of guiding him, left him more confused, more lost.

Discouragement was starting to set in. Was he not meant to navigate this sea? Was the knowledge too vast for him to comprehend? The questions, laced with self-doubt, started to cloud his mind. But then, he remembered Sage's words, "To progress, to innovate, one must be open to absorbing knowledge, adapting to new information, and never ceasing to learn."

Taking a deep breath, Alexander steadied his shaking hands on the boat's edges. He looked at the compass, still pulsating gently, a subtle reminder of Sage's presence, her guidance. He decided not to rush, not to let the vastness of the sea overwhelm him. It was not a race, but a journey. A journey of learning, of understanding, and of growth.

With renewed determination, he steered the boat deeper into the sea, ready to face whatever challenges lay ahead. Alexander knew the journey would not be easy, but he also knew he was ready to take on the learning curve, to face the fear of the unknown, and to embrace the voyage of continuous learning.

Suddenly, there was a flicker in the air before him, and Sage's image appeared. The elderly woman's spectral form looked as calm and collected as ever, her soft voice carrying over the gentle lull of the sea.

"Alexander," she began, her eyes twinkling with a secret, "in your heart, you carry the desire to learn, an innate compass that guides you towards growth. But for this sea, you'll need something a bit more... tangible."

From the ethereal folds of her cloak, Sage drew out a gleaming compass. It was simple, elegant, its needle a vibrant silver that seemed to dance under the Sea's luminescent glow.

"This compass," she held it out to him, her ghostly fingers passing through the device, "isn't ordinary. It will not point north, east, south, or west. Instead, it will lead you to where you need to go, to the knowledge you need the most. But remember, it works on your desire to learn, your thirst for understanding. Do not let it falter, Alexander."

With those words, Sage's form flickered once more and then vanished, leaving behind the levitating compass. Alexander reached out hesitantly, his hand closing around the cool metal. A surge of warmth spread through him, a feeling of connection, of purpose. The needle, which had been spinning wildly, slowly started to settle, pointing towards a particularly bright cluster of books in the distance.

With the compass in his grasp, Alexander felt a renewed sense of purpose. His heart pounded in his chest as he steered the boat in the direction indicated. This compass was more than just a tool; it was a manifestation of his desire to learn, a tangible beacon guiding him through this sea of knowledge.

The compass in Alexander's grasp was no ordinary navigational tool; it pulsed with a life of its own, guiding him through the Sea of Lifelong Learning. As he followed its lead, the sea began to reveal its secrets. Each book, podcast, and course emerged from the waves not as an obstacle but as an invitation, an opportunity for exploration and understanding.

One day, a hefty tome titled "The Histories of the World Beyond" floated toward him. Hesitant but curious, Alexander opened the book to find detailed accounts of civilizations, cultures, and innovations he'd never imagined. His eyes widened with each page he turned, his mind buzzing with newfound knowledge.

In the quiet of the night, he'd listen to the podcasts whispering tales of people's experiences, their triumphs, their failures. One particular story of a man who turned his small village into a thriving city using innovative methods resonated with him. He found himself revisiting the story, gleaning insights and inspiration.

He dived into a course titled "Harnessing the Power of Change," where he discovered concepts and strategies that could aid his quest to transform Stagnant Shores. The course was challenging, but the compass provided guidance, leading him to the right resources, helping him grasp the complex ideas.

With each passing day, the initial overwhelm was replaced with exhilaration. The sea, once a daunting expanse, now felt like a treasure chest, filled with pearls of wisdom and gems of knowledge. He no longer saw the sea as an adversary but as a mentor, challenging him, pushing him towards growth.

The realization was profound. This sea, vast and deep, mirrored the journey of continuous learning. There was always more to discover, more to understand. It embodied the idea that knowledge is not a destination but an ongoing journey.

This compass-led voyage through the Sea of Lifelong Learning was molding Alexander, his outlook evolving with every wave he navigated. As he sailed deeper, he felt equipped, ready for the challenges that lay ahead, his heart filled with the joy of learning and a resolve strengthened by understanding.

Navigating through the Sea of Lifelong Learning proved to be an enlightening odyssey for Alexander. He had faced challenges, had been bewildered by the vastness of knowledge that the sea represented, but with the compass in hand, he had journeyed on. As the days turned into weeks, Alexander found that his once disoriented confusion had metamorphosed into an organized curiosity.

The compass, a symbol of his desire to learn, had become his trusted guide. It led him towards the knowledge that he was ready to understand, insights that broadened his perspectives, and lessons that tested his resilience. He discovered concepts he'd never known, engaged with theories that challenged his beliefs, and stumbled upon stories that inspired him.

One afternoon, as he steered his boat through a wave of books, a particular volume caught his attention. The book was named "The Power of Community," its pages filled with instances of communities transforming through collaborative efforts and shared learning. Alexander was captivated, he spent hours reading, imagining the potential of such transformation in Stagnant Shores.

As he journeyed through the sea, his understanding of learning evolved. Learning was not merely the acquisition of knowledge. It was understanding, it was questioning, it was growing. It was not a race to know it all, but a journey that embraced the joy of discovery, the satisfaction of understanding, and the resilience in the face of complexity.

This voyage through the Sea of Lifelong Learning had revealed to Alexander a version of himself he'd always aspired to be - a relentless learner, a curious seeker, a resolute changer. The sea was no longer a daunting obstacle; it was a testament to his journey, a reflection of his growth.

As the sight of the Sea of Lifelong Learning faded into the horizon, Alexander felt a sense of accomplishment. He had navigated through the sea, had faced its challenges, had embraced its lessons. But more importantly, he had emerged as a beacon of lifelong learning, his mind enriched, his spirit invigorated, and his resolve stronger than ever.

His transformation was mirrored in his confident stance, in his thoughtful gaze that looked out at the horizon, anticipating the journey ahead. The sea had taught him the importance of continuous learning, the essence of intellectual growth. But the journey was far from over, and Alexander knew it.

As the winds of knowledge continued to propel him forward, he carried with him a deep-seated understanding - learning was not a phase but a lifelong pursuit, a journey that had no end, only new beginnings. The sea had prepared him for the voyage ahead, had equipped him with the mindset of a lifelong learner. And as he looked ahead, NexGen Island was one step closer.

"Bring on the challenges," he whispered to the wind, a determined smile playing on his lips, "I am ready."

As the last ripples of the Sea of Lifelong Learning faded into the distance, Alexander took a moment to reflect. He had navigated through a sea of knowledge, each wave, each current presenting a new lesson, a new perspective. It wasn't merely about getting through the sea; it was about the transformation he felt within. He could feel it - the spark of curiosity had turned into a flame, illuminating his thoughts, shaping his actions. He looked at the compass, its needle steady, a symbol of his journey so far and a reminder of the continual quest for learning. He had conquered the Sea of Lifelong Learning and had emerged not just victorious but enlightened.

Drawing closer to the Forest of Human Behavior, the enormity of his upcoming journey started to sink in. The forest, with its vastness, echoed the complexities of human emotions and behaviors. It wasn't just a physical landscape but a representation of the human psyche, and Alexander was about to delve into it.

He stared at the densely packed trees, their branches stretching out like arms welcoming him into their depths. There was a sense of anticipation in the air as Alexander looked ahead, a flutter of excitement, a ripple of uncertainty. As he approached, his gaze fell upon a peculiarly shaped tree. It stood taller and more twisted than the others, its silhouette stark against the sky.

In that tree, Alexander saw his first challenge. It was a mirror, reflecting his fear and anticipation. What mysteries lay within the forest? What understanding awaited him?

As he readied himself to step into the forest, the compass in his hand felt heavier. The Sea of Lifelong Learning had prepared him, but this was a different challenge altogether. He was on the precipice of a journey of introspection, a deep dive into the labyrinth of emotions. With a final look at the vast sea behind him and the towering forest ahead, Alexander took a deep breath. He was not just stepping into the Forest of Human Behavior; he was stepping into a new chapter of his life.

"Here we go," he whispered, his heart pounding in his chest. The forest loomed large, holding secrets, holding challenges, holding growth. And Alexander was ready to uncover them all. As he neared the shore, his grip tightened around the compass. The Forest of Human Behavior was his next stop in his journey to NexGen Island. The stage was set. The adventure was about to intensify.

As Alexander stepped onto the shore, he was filled with a renewed sense of purpose. The forest awaited, and with it, a journey into the mind and soul. But for now, the forest stood silent, its secrets safe within. A sense of anticipation hung in the air. This was the calm before the storm, the pause before the plunge, the breath before the dive. Alexander was on the brink of a new adventure, and he was ready to face it head-on. The journey to NexGen Island had truly begun.

Chapter 3
The Forest of Human Behavior

As the waters of the Sea of Lifelong Learning calmed and the outlines of a dense forest began to emerge from the mist, Alexander found himself reminiscing about the challenges he had just overcome. The sea, with its waves of books, podcasts, and courses, was not just a physical barrier to cross, but also a testament to the importance of continuous learning and growth.

He recalled the confusion that first consumed him when he plunged into the depths of the sea, confronted by an overwhelming surge of knowledge. The realization that knowledge was not a burden but a tool for navigating life's complexities was hard-won.

His fingers traced the compass gifted by Sage, the metal cool against his skin. Its symbolism had made all the difference. It was not the direction of the compass needle that mattered, but rather the hunger for learning it represented. With it, he had navigated the sea, deciphering the intricacies of the resources that emerged from the depths. Books that opened his mind to new ideas, podcasts that filled his ears with diverse perspectives, and courses that challenged his understanding of the world.

In the face of these challenges, Sage's wisdom had been his guiding light. It was she who had explained the significance of the Sea of Lifelong Learning. "A mind that is hungry for knowledge," she had said, "can cross any sea, scale any mountain, and traverse any forest." Those words reverberated in his mind as he bid the sea a silent goodbye and steered his vessel towards the silhouette of trees looming ahead.

As the sun marked its peak in the azure sky, Alexander's journey through the Sea of Lifelong Learning came to a victorious end. But this triumph was not an end in itself. Instead, it marked the beginning of a new chapter in his journey to NexGen Island.

Now, as he approached the Forest of Human Behavior, he felt better prepared to face what lay ahead, the lessons from the sea still fresh in his mind. The journey had shown him that to learn was to grow, and to grow was to move closer to his ultimate goal.

The transition from the tranquil sea to the threshold of the sprawling Forest of Human Behavior was abrupt, almost jarring. As Alexander's boat gently nudged the leafy banks, he found himself gazing at a living, breathing organism of ancient trees and vibrant foliage. A symphony of nature's sounds filled the air - rustling leaves, whispering winds, and creatures hidden within the forest's depths.

***

Stepping onto the forest floor, the cool, moist earth squelched under his boots. The scent of damp earth and fresh leaves was a sharp contrast to the salty sea air he had grown accustomed to. Alexander's heart pounded with a mix of exhilaration and trepidation as he ventured deeper into the forest, the shadows growing denser with each step.

The Forest of Human Behavior was not just a physical location but a labyrinth of complexities and intricacies. It was like walking into a crowded room where everyone was engaged in conversation, but instead of words, emotions were the language. A sudden gust of wind seemed like a collective sigh of the forest; a rustle of leaves akin to whispered secrets.

The deeper he ventured, the more he felt the forest's pulse. It was a world teeming with life and constant interaction. However, understanding the ebb and flow of these interactions was the real challenge. Alexander soon realized that each creature, each rustling leaf, even the shifting shadows, all communicated something essential - but the meanings were not clear to him.

The sense of disorientation crept up on him slowly. Each step forward seemed to take him deeper into a maze of confusion. His previous journey on the sea had been a challenge, but there he had his compass of lifelong learning. But how could he navigate a place where emotions were the guiding forces, and no physical tool could aid his understanding?

The reality of his situation weighed heavily on Alexander. His heartbeat echoed in his ears, a physical manifestation of his inner turmoil. Yet, despite the overwhelming uncertainty, he couldn't help but marvel at the forest's raw beauty and complexity. It was a puzzle waiting to be solved, and he was determined to decipher it. As he navigated through the maze of trees, the first lesson of the Forest of Human Behavior was dawning upon him - understanding others starts with understanding oneself.

***

Lost. It was an unsettling feeling, a gnawing sense of uncertainty that wrapped around Alexander like a thick, oppressive fog. He had been wandering through the Forest of Human Behavior for what felt like days, the dense canopy of trees disorienting his sense of time and direction.

Alexander had faced physical challenges before. Navigating the Sea of Lifelong Learning had been daunting, yes, but it was a struggle he could understand, a challenge he could prepare for. The forest, however, was a different beast altogether. It was unpredictable, its whispers alluring yet deceptive, its inhabitants a mystery.

Every rustling leaf, every animal sound, every shift in the wind seemed to be a sign, a hint of something he needed to understand. Yet, the more he tried to decipher the forest's language, the more confused he became. He felt like he was trying to read a book in a language he didn't understand.

Encountering the forest's inhabitants added another layer of complexity. Creatures of all shapes and sizes roamed the forest, each one displaying unique behaviors and responses. Some creatures were approachable, meeting his gaze with curious eyes, while others scurried away at his approach. There were creatures whose roars echoed menacingly through the trees and others that communicated in soft, melodic tunes. It was a living, breathing mosaic of behaviors, a vast spectrum of reactions that painted a vivid picture of diversity.

One particular encounter with a creature, a bird with plumage of iridescent colors, exemplified his struggle. As he extended his hand in friendship, the bird recoiled, ruffling its feathers in what seemed like fear or anger. Alexander was left standing, hand outstretched, a sense of rejection sweeping over him.

But there was no time to dwell on feelings of dejection. Each interaction, each rejection or acceptance, was a lesson he had to decipher.

His instinct to react was replaced by an urgent need to understand, to comprehend the why behind every reaction, every behavior.

Alexander realized he was not just lost geographically but emotionally and mentally. He was lost in the labyrinth of understanding and interpreting behaviors. The forest was challenging him, prodding him to go beyond his instincts, beyond the surface of behaviors, pushing him to grasp the underlying emotions and motivations. It was daunting, confusing, and at times overwhelming.

And yet, despite the confusion, despite the sense of being lost, Alexander could not ignore the rising spark of fascination within him. It was a puzzle, a riddle that seemed impossible yet enticing. He knew he had to persist, to strive and learn from the forest. The path was difficult, the journey arduous, but Alexander, driven by the desire to understand, pressed on. The Forest of Human Behavior was living up to its reputation, presenting him with challenges he had never foreseen, pushing him to the brink of his intellectual and emotional capacities.

***

The disorienting maze of the Forest of Human Behavior left Alexander bewildered. He stood in the midst of this lush, living labyrinth, the hum of the forest's inhabitants filling his ears, and a sense of isolation creeping over him. His thoughts circled back to Sage's words, ones she had shared under a star-lit sky, their resonance echoing now within him.

"Emotional intelligence," Sage had said, her voice a gentle murmur against the rustling of the wind, "It's more than just intellect, Alexander. It's the ability to perceive, understand, and manage our emotions, as well as those of others around us."

At that moment, beneath the moonlit sky, Alexander had been unable to grasp the true depth of Sage's words. But now, within the heart of this alien forest, her counsel seemed to hold a profound significance.

As he observed the creatures around him, their behaviors shifting like the wind - sometimes cautious, other times hostile - he started to recognize the emotions driving their actions. Fear, caution, joy, curiosity... they were expressions of their internal states, their experiences, their essence.

Alexander felt a stir of understanding. The forest, in all its complexity and diversity, was a mirror to the realm of human interactions. Each creature, each behavior, held meaning beyond the surface. They were akin to the people back in Stagnant Shores, each carrying a world within, a symphony of emotions, dreams, fears, and desires.

Gradually, Alexander began to see the forest not as an adversary but as a mentor. Its lessons were not written in books or spoken in words, but were there in the rustle of leaves, the call of birds, the dance of shadows. They were in the quiet moments of observation and introspection, waiting to be discovered, understood, and appreciated.

Embracing this realization, Alexander felt a change within him. Fear and confusion gave way to empathy and understanding. The forest, once a formidable foe, transformed into a guide, leading him towards a deeper understanding of emotional intelligence.

This new perspective didn't make the path through the Forest of Human Behavior any less challenging, but it did make Alexander better equipped to face it. With every step, he grew more attuned to the forest's rhythm, its subtle cues becoming lessons, its challenges turning into opportunities for growth. Sage's words had ignited a spark within him, illuminating his path, and transforming his voyage into a journey of learning and self-discovery.

The Forest of Human Behavior was no longer a trial to endure but an exploration of the self, a testament to the power of empathy, understanding, and emotional intelligence. As Alexander delved deeper into this journey, he was not just navigating a forest; he was traversing the landscape of his own understanding, growing with every step he took.

***

An eerie calm enveloped the Forest of Human Behavior as night fell, the once cacophonous hubbub of the day reduced to an anticipatory hush. Alexander, encamped under the sprawling branches of an old tree, couldn't help but feel the profound shift in the forest's atmosphere. The symphony of the forest was quiet, but not silent. Each rustle of leaves, every distant animal call, was a thread in the intricate tapestry of this unique landscape.

He remembered an encounter from earlier in the day. He'd accidentally ventured too close to a bird's nest. Its sharp, shrill squawking was an alarm, a boundary being set. At first, Alexander had been startled, viewing the creature as a threat. But as he stood still, observing the bird's frantic circling around its nest, an understanding dawned on him. The bird wasn't an enemy, but a parent protecting its young. Its aggression wasn't unprovoked hostility but born out of fear for its offspring. Recognizing this, Alexander had slowly backed away, allowing the bird to calm down and return to its nest.

It was Sage's words that guided him in these moments of tension. "Every creature," she'd said, "speaks in its own emotional language.

Learn to understand it, not just observe it." With this wisdom in mind, Alexander didn't just see the bird's actions; he understood its emotions. The bird's relief when he backed away was a testament to his first successful 'conversation' in this emotional language.

With each day, Alexander found himself becoming more attuned to this silent dialogue. He saw the playful chase of two squirrels in a different light, recognizing the joy in their swift, agile movements. He could understand the focused patience of a predator lying in wait, respecting its strategic silence.

These lessons of emotional intelligence were challenging, taking him out of his comfort zone. However, each interaction, each observation, peeled back a layer of the Forest of Human Behavior. The seemingly chaotic array of creatures were no longer just part of the scenery; they became his teachers, his guides, imparting lessons of empathy, resilience, and respect for boundaries.

***

In the solitude of the forest night, Alexander reflected on his progress. He'd begun his journey with a vague understanding of emotional intelligence, and now, it was becoming his lifeline, his compass guiding him through the dense labyrinth of the forest. The Forest of Human Behavior was no longer a terrifying unknown; it was an open book, every page a new lesson to learn and appreciate.

Undeniably, the Forest of Human Behavior was a world unto itself, brimming with a multitude of creatures, each with its own behaviors, emotions, and social structures. But Alexander wasn't walking through it as a mere spectator anymore. He was now an active participant, interpreting behaviors, understanding emotions, and making connections.

One particularly cold evening, as he nestled against the towering trunk of a tree, he found himself face to face with a formidable wolf. Its lips curled back in a growl, revealing a set of sharp teeth. Fear sparked in Alexander's heart, his breath hitching as the primal fear of a predator surged through him.

Then, Sage's words whispered in his mind, "Alexander, emotion isn't a one-way street. It's a dialogue, a dance between two beings." Taking a deep, shaky breath, he slowly withdrew, his palms turned upwards in a universal gesture of peace. The wolf, after a tense moment, relaxed its aggressive stance, silently slinking back into the darkness of the forest.

Breathing a sigh of relief, Alexander muttered under his breath, "Thank you, Sage. Your wisdom saved me tonight."

***

A few days later, he found himself amid a troop of monkeys. Their incessant chatter, erratic movements, and piercing cries initially set his nerves on edge. However, remembering Sage's guidance, Alexander decided to observe before reacting.

"They're not aggressive, just social and protective. You're the stranger here, Alexander," he reminded himself. Maintaining a respectful distance, he moved cautiously, causing minimal disruption to their habitat. To his surprise, the monkeys' shrieking ebbed, their frenzied movements slowed, and the troop continued their activities, paying Alexander no mind.

"They understood," Alexander exclaimed, a broad smile spreading across his face, "They understood my intention. They know I mean no harm."

The compass of emotional intelligence Sage had given him was leading him on a journey of self-discovery and growth. He was learning to observe, understand, and respect the emotional territories of others.

The forest was no longer a dense, indecipherable mystery. Instead, it was an open book, narrating tales of cooperation, survival, and communication. Alexander wasn't merely wandering through the forest; he was dancing with it, engaging in a silent dialogue with its inhabitants.

"Who knew understanding could be such a powerful tool," Alexander mused aloud one evening, gazing at the setting sun, "Sage was right; we're all connected in this dance of emotion and behavior."

***

Alexander had spent many sunrises and sunsets in the Forest of Human Behavior, each day a lesson, each encounter a story. Every creature, every interaction had taught him something valuable about emotional intelligence.

One day, after he'd managed to negotiate his way through a territorial dispute between two opposing groups of forest creatures, Alexander sat by the riverside, watching the water flow with a thoughtful expression.

"I've learnt more about emotions and behavior here than I ever did in Stagnant Shores," Alexander admitted aloud, his voice echoing in the stillness. "It's like...like the creatures here understand the dance of behavior, the rhythm of emotion." A pause. "Sage was right. Emotional intelligence isn't just about understanding others—it's about understanding oneself too."

A sense of satisfaction washed over him, and he realized, he'd made it. He'd successfully navigated the Forest of Human Behavior. With newfound knowledge and a compass guiding him, he'd managed to not only survive but thrive.

The forest that had once seemed so alien and intimidating was now a source of wisdom and understanding. It had shown him a mirror to his own emotions, his strengths, his weaknesses. And in understanding them, Alexander had learned to steer his path better, to read the unspoken language of emotions, to respect the boundaries of others while asserting his own.

Armed with these insights, he stood on the edge of the forest one crisp morning, his eyes catching the first glimpse of what lay ahead. The sight took his breath away.

Massive, snow-capped peaks rose in the distance, their formidable size dwarfing everything around them. A sense of awe washed over Alexander as he beheld the Mountains of Modern Tools. They were unlike anything he'd ever seen in Stagnant Shores.

"This is the next stage of my journey," Alexander whispered, a hint of nervousness creeping into his voice. He looked back at the forest one last time, a silent thank you escaping his lips for the lessons it had imparted. Then, squaring his shoulders, he began his trek towards the mountains.

"Mountains are climbed not in leaps, but one step at a time," Sage had once said during their evening conversations. The memory brought a small smile to Alexander's face. "Well, Sage," he said to the wind, "It's time to take the first step."

With a deep breath, Alexander took a step towards the Mountains of Modern Tools, his heart pounding in his chest. His journey had just begun. The sea and the forest had equipped him with knowledge and emotional intelligence. Now, it was time to learn about the modern tools that could enable change.

His mind buzzed with anticipation. The trials he'd faced, the lessons he'd learned, all were leading him to this moment. As he looked at the vast expanse of snow and stone, he couldn't help but wonder about the challenges and adventures that lay ahead.

As the sun began its descent, casting long shadows over the landscape, Alexander set up camp, preparing himself for the journey ahead. The wind carried whispers of the trials to come, but Alexander felt ready.

"Bring it on, Mountains of Modern Tools," Alexander muttered to himself, his gaze steady on the towering peaks. "I'm ready to learn. I'm ready to grow."

As he wrapped himself in his blanket, under the starry blanket of the night sky, Alexander fell asleep with dreams of the mountains. Tomorrow, he would step into a new adventure, climb new heights, and unlock new learnings. Tomorrow, he would start his ascent.

And so, as the night blanketed the world in its quiet serenity, Alexander slept soundly, the Mountains of Modern Tools a silent sentinel against the starlit sky, holding the promise of the challenges, lessons, and adventures that awaited him.

Chapter 4

The Mountains of Modern Tools

E merging from the dense foliage of the Forest of Human Behavior, Alexander was welcomed by a landscape vastly different from the one he had left behind. Towering before him were the Mountains of Modern Tools. The mammoth peaks seemed to reach for the sky, their jagged edges veined with the glow of what seemed like neon circuitry. Against the backdrop of the azure sky, they looked both inviting and daunting.

The mountains appeared as a massive interlocking puzzle, an intricate mesh of moving parts and pulsating light. They were akin to a colossal machine, humming and buzzing, echoing with the rhythm of unseen cogs and wheels. It was like nothing Alexander had seen before, a testament to an advanced, almost alien world of innovation and technology.

Standing at the foot of the imposing mountains, Alexander felt a shiver of uncertainty. He had conquered the Sea of Lifelong Learning, traversed the Forest of Human Behavior, but this... this was a different beast altogether. The scale of his task dawned on him, casting a shadow of doubt. Would his wisdom and emotional intelligence be enough to navigate these towering pinnacles of modernity?

But amidst the sea of doubts, a spark of awe ignited in his heart. This was a symbol of human innovation, a representation of how far mankind had come. These mountains stood as a testament to the power of knowledge and learning, the fruits of a civilization's relentless pursuit of progress.

As the last rays of the setting sun painted the peaks in hues of crimson and gold, Alexander took a deep breath. The journey ahead was daunting, but the mountains held an irresistible allure. They symbolized a world of opportunities, the potential to learn, grow, and transform. And Alexander was ready to scale their heights, ready to embrace the lessons they had to offer.

***

As Alexander stood marveling at the grandeur of the mountains, a soft rustling sound pulled him back. Turning around, he found Sage, her silhouette framed by the setting sun, a mysterious glow radiating from her hand.

"Alexander," she called out, her voice dancing with an unusual excitement. Alexander walked up to her, curiosity gleaming in his eyes. "In the mountains of modernity, the tools you need will differ from those in the forest or the sea," she said, unveiling a strange object that she had been holding.

In her palm, Sage held what looked like a disc of glass, the size of a pocket watch. It was remarkably thin, and the setting sun's rays reflected off its surface, scattering kaleidoscopic hues. With a single tap from her finger, the seemingly innocuous disc came to life, bathing their faces in a warm, blue light. Projected above the disc was a three-dimensional topographical map, meticulously detailed, with pulsating lines and markers.

"This is more than just a map, Alexander," Sage began, her gaze locked onto the mesmerizing projection. "This is an AI-powered guide. It is a creation of intellect and intuition, a testament to the power of modern tools."

She proceeded to explain its workings. The map was dynamic, it evolved with every passing moment, updating itself based on the terrain and the climber's progress. It advised on safe paths, warned of dangerous terrains, calculated rest periods based on the climber's fatigue, and even suggested the most efficient routes.

But what intrigued Alexander the most was that it was not just an advisor. It was a learner. "It learns from you, Alexander," Sage explained, a spark in her eyes. "It will adapt to your climbing style, your pace, your strengths, and weaknesses. It embodies the essence of modern tools – to aid, to learn, and to evolve."

Listening to Sage, Alexander was awestruck. The map symbolized what the mountains stood for: innovation, progress, and an endless pursuit of knowledge. It was a tool, a guide, and a companion.

Receiving the AI-powered map from Sage, Alexander felt a surge of confidence. The task ahead was colossal, but he was not alone. He had a powerful ally, a testament to mankind's ingenuity. This was not just about reaching the summit; it was about understanding the symbiotic relationship between man and modern tools. Alexander, with the AI map in his hand and determination in his heart, was ready to embark on this new challenge.

***

With the glowing AI map clutched in his hand, Alexander approached the rocky base of the first peak. The ascent started gently, but it wasn't long before the terrain became challenging. He was in a world of verticality, of sheer rock faces and gravel-strewn paths that threatened to slide under his every step.

His first setback came in the form of a sudden landslide. Rocks, loosened by his scrambling, tumbled down the slope. His heart pounded in his chest as he scrambled to a safer spot, avoiding the cascade of stones. Shaken, he paused, taking a moment to steady his breath.

Looking at the AI map, he noticed that it had already updated. The area where the landslide occurred was now marked with a red hazard sign. A sense of relief washed over him. This tool was not just reactive; it was predictive, capable of protecting him from dangers he couldn't foresee.

Taking a deep breath, Alexander continued his ascent, this time with renewed caution. He began to learn how to read the map better, interpreting its signals and warnings. With each small victory, each successful navigation through a dangerous patch, his trust in the map grew.

***

One day, he found himself standing before a seemingly insurmountable vertical cliff. His heart sank; he had never faced such a steep climb. However, the map suggested a less visible path that wound around the side of the mountain. Despite his initial hesitation, Alexander decided to trust the AI guide.

Following the AI map's directions, he discovered a hidden path through a narrow crevice. It was a tough squeeze, but it led him to a less steep incline on the other side of the mountain. He could not help but marvel at the map's precision and intuition, appreciating how it was learning his capabilities and limitations.

As the days turned into weeks, Alexander's initial struggles began to lessen. He had a greater understanding of the AI map and more faith in its guidance. His relationship with the map transformed from mere dependence to a true partnership. Through every slip, every setback, and every victory, he was not just climbing a mountain. He was learning the immense potential of modern tools, the power they held, and the collaboration they fostered.

Every day on the mountain, Alexander learned something new, not just about the terrain but about his companion, the AI-powered map. The tool became more than just a means to an end, transforming into an educator, a guide, a silent partner in his quest.

"Warning: unstable ledge ahead. Suggested route: redirect 30 degrees northwest," the map vibrated in his hand one day. Alexander squinted at the suggested path on the screen, a treacherous trail leading away from the ledge. With a determined nod, he veered northwest, and minutes later, a resonating rumble filled the air as the ledge collapsed.

"Good call," Alexander murmured to the map, patting its screen in silent gratitude.

Another day, during a particularly steep ascent, the map pinged: "Suggested climbing pattern: zigzag ascent for optimal energy conservation." Alexander paused, considering the advice. Following the map's guidance, he began his zigzag climb. As he climbed, he felt his exhaustion lessening, his movements becoming more efficient. Reaching the top, he let out a triumphant laugh. "You're a brilliant teacher," he exclaimed, holding up the map to the mountain peak.

In this AI map, Alexander found more than a tool. He found a mentor, one that understood his environment better than he did, and more importantly, knew how to use that knowledge for his benefit. The power of modern tools, he realized, wasn't merely in their advanced capabilities. It was in their potential to empower the user, to enhance their skills, and to transform challenges into opportunities.

Guided by the AI-powered map, Alexander charted his journey higher and higher, each step marked by new triumphs. The mountains, once a daunting symbol of the unknown, became his training ground.

With each alert from the map, he made another decision – to trust the device, to adapt his course, to overcome the challenge in his path. Over time, he found himself anticipating the map's advice, even incorporating its insights before they arrived.

***

On a particularly challenging afternoon, as the sun beat down relentlessly and the path seemed nearly vertical, Alexander paused. He was out of breath, his muscles screamed for rest, but looking at his AI map, he saw the next rest stop was still some distance away.

"No stopping till we get there," he told himself aloud, voice echoing against the stark mountain walls. The map, humming softly in his hand, was showing a way around a looming rock face. His path lay upwards, and he trusted the map to guide him.

As he navigated around the rock face, finding handholds and ledges where he thought none existed, a new realization dawned upon him. This tool, the map, was more than just a device. It was an extension of himself, amplifying his abilities and compensating for his shortcomings. It wasn't replacing his skills, but rather enhancing them, enabling him to climb heights he never could have on his own.

Alexander reached the rest stop as the sun began its descent, casting long shadows over the rugged terrain. He sank down on a mossy rock, a triumphant smile creeping onto his weary face. Holding the AI map in front of him, he declared, "We did it!" His voice echoed back to him in the crisp mountain air, a testament to his victory. The importance of modern tools had never been clearer to Alexander. They weren't just devices. They were partners, collaborators, teachers. And they held the key to overcoming the seemingly impossible.

As dusk fell, casting dramatic shadows across the mountain landscape, Alexander settled at a plateau, the perfect rest point after a grueling climb. His gaze swept over the terrain he had traversed, each rocky crag and narrow ledge a testament to his unwavering determination and the AI map's guiding light.

Under the shimmering stars, he held the map, its glow mirroring the new understanding in his eyes. The tool was more than just an object; it was a symbol of humanity's potential, a testament to the empowering force of modern innovation.

***

With the arrival of dawn, a new challenge beckoned. As the sun bled into the sky, painting it with hues of fiery red and soft pink, the contours of the next part of his journey unfurled before him. Beyond the daunting silhouette of the Mountains of Modern Tools lay an expanse that glittered like a mosaic under the morning light - the Valley of Collaboration and Innovation.

Packing his gear, Alexander felt a coil of anticipation twine with a thread of anxiety within him. The Valley was a realm of uncertainties, its mystery as intriguing as it was daunting. But he was not the same man who had left Stagnant Shores; he had grown, evolved, and conquered.

He glanced at the AI map, its familiar glow steady and reassuring. It was more than a tool now; it was a symbol of his journey, a testament to the power of perseverance and innovation. His gaze settled on the vast expanse of the Valley. "We have mountains behind us, and a valley ahead," he murmured to himself, a determined spark in his eyes.

With a last glance at the mountain range that had tested his mettle, Alexander began his descent. The Mountains of Modern Tools stood tall in the breaking dawn, a monument to his accomplishments, and a silent vow of the challenges that lay ahead in the Valley of Collaboration and Innovation. A new chapter was about to unfold in his quest to reach NexGen Island.

Chapter 5
The Valley of Collaboration and Innovation

A lexander's journey through the Mountains of Modern Tools had been an expedition of discovery and transformation. The high peaks that once seemed insurmountable were now behind him, conquered with perseverance and the guiding light of an AI-powered map. His heart pounded in his chest as he thought back to his first steps, the uncertainty that had clouded his mind.

"Alexander," Sage's voice echoed in his memory, her wise eyes twinkling, "This map is more than just a tool, it's a symbol of the power of modern technology."

Alexander had grappled with the alien technology, his hands fumbling as he deciphered the map's intricate features. His initial steps had been hesitant, each small victory overshadowed by setbacks. The mountains were unforgiving, their steep cliffs a formidable opponent.

However, he persisted. With each failure, he learned, adapted, and evolved. The map, which had once seemed so foreign, started making sense. Alexander could almost hear Sage's encouraging words, "The power of modern tools is transformative, Alexander, but only when used correctly."

Soon, he was climbing higher, progressing further. The peaks that seemed daunting were now within his reach. His heart was full of triumph as he reached a rest point, the AI map firmly clutched in his hand. The experience was humbling and transformative.

Alexander stood tall, looking back at the towering Mountains of Modern Tools. They were a testament to his journey and the transformative power of modern tools. He felt a new confidence, a sense of empowerment. He was not the same person who had first set foot on this journey.

His thoughts shifted towards the future, a spark of anticipation lighting up his eyes. As he descended into the valley, he wondered what lessons awaited him next in his quest to reach NexGen Island.

***

As Alexander set foot into the valley, his senses were assailed by a veritable orchestra of activity. The Valley of Collaboration and Innovation was unlike anything he had ever seen. Colorful creatures fluttered about, their wings sparkling in the sunlight as they moved in unison, like a well-choreographed dance. On the ground, sturdy beasts lumbered, carving paths through the lush greenery, their grunts and roars a testament to their hard work.

A sense of purposeful chaos reigned, each creature, despite their apparent differences, working in harmony, contributing to the valley's vibrant ecosystem. The air buzzed with an energy that Alexander found both exhilarating and overwhelming.

The sight was spellbinding, the valley pulsating with life, each creature an embodiment of a unique skill, all moving, creating, innovating together. Alexander, rooted at the entrance, couldn't help but be in awe of the dynamism of the scene unfolding before him. However, beneath the awe was an undercurrent of trepidation. How could he, a single person, interact and collaborate in this vast, bustling valley? Despite his uncertainties, the marvel of the spectacle before him steeled his resolve. This was his challenge, his path to walk, and he was prepared to step forth.

As Alexander ventured deeper into the valley, a collection of creatures came into view. Each one was markedly different from the other, each creature representing a distinct skillset, their unique abilities contributing to the dynamism of the valley.

The fast-paced Flutterers with iridescent wings seemed to represent communication, flitting from one creature to the other, their chirps and tweets resonating through the valley. The towering Builders, their bodies made of sturdy stones, signified strength and persistence. On the valley floor, the tiny Tinkers, with their nimble fingers, represented innovation, their quick movements assembling, disassembling, and reassembling objects in the blink of an eye.

Observing them, Alexander felt a pang of confusion. Each creature was so different, so specialized in their tasks, that he couldn't fathom how to guide and work with them. The idea was daunting, as if he had stumbled upon a puzzle with pieces too intricate for him to comprehend. He wondered how he could bridge the gap between them, how to blend into their harmony, and contribute to the valley's rhythm. But in that bewilderment, Alexander also felt a growing sense of determination. He realized that understanding this diverse group and collaborating with them was the key to navigating the Valley of

Collaboration and Innovation. The challenge lay before him, and he was ready to embrace it.

***

As Alexander grappled with his uncertainty, he heard Sage's voice echo in his mind, a guiding beacon in his moment of doubt. "Alexander, remember, the essence of collaboration and innovation lies in diversity. Each creature here possesses a unique skill, a different perspective. Together, they create a tapestry of potential."

Her words hung in the air as Alexander pondered their meaning. He glanced at the bird, its keen eye focused on building, at the multi-armed creature, demonstrating a mastery of multitasking, and the group of small critters, their unity creating strength. Could they come together for a common purpose?

"In the center of the valley," Sage's voice continued, "there's an ancient structure, a symbol of unity. But it's in disrepair now. Alexander, I propose a challenge: Guide these creatures in restoring it."

Alexander looked to the center of the valley, where a towering structure stood. It was grand, its architecture intricate, yet it was evident that it had seen better days. Its once-majestic form was now marred with broken pieces, a testament to the passage of time.

He turned back to the creatures, their eyes on him, expectant. Despite his apprehension, a spark of determination flickered in his eyes. Guiding these creatures, with their diverse skills and abilities, to restore the ancient structure—this was his challenge. This was his chance to experience the power of collaboration and innovation first-hand.

***

With Sage's words echoing in his mind, Alexander took a deep breath, his eyes focused on the diverse group of creatures before him. It was time to put theory into practice.

"Alexander," Sage had said, "you'll have to guide them. Collaboration is not about controlling but about coordinating. Understand their strengths, help them understand each other. Remember, they're as different as they are important."

Alexander approached the creatures, his voice steady despite the apprehension inside him, "We have a task ahead. I believe we can tackle it together."

The Flutterers stopped their conversation, the Builders paused in their actions, and the Tinkers looked up from their projects. They watched this stranger amongst them, waiting for his next words.

"I don't claim to know how things work here, but I see strength, communication, and innovation among us," Alexander continued, meeting their gazes, "Together, we can overcome any challenge."

The days that followed were rife with trials and errors. The initial attempts at collaboration were far from smooth. Misunderstandings and miscommunications led to confusion. However, Alexander's persistent attempts at understanding each creature's skills and encouraging them to work together began to pay off.

Slowly, a pattern emerged. The Flutterers started delivering messages more effectively, helping to coordinate efforts. The Builders understood the importance of their strength in implementing the plans. The Tinkers, on the other hand, began to innovate more efficiently, their tiny hands crafting tools and solutions to problems they faced.

Each day, each interaction was a lesson for Alexander. The dynamics of teamwork began to unfurl before him, and he found himself evolving, learning, and adapting. His leadership was not about command and control; instead, it was about guidance, understanding, and mutual respect. The valley started to buzz with a newfound synergy, the energy palpable, the momentum unstoppable.

***

Under the starry night, the last piece of the monumental structure was set into place. A cheer echoed through the valley as the creatures and Alexander admired their collective creation. The once-decaying structure now stood proudly, a beacon of unity and collaboration amidst the Valley of Collaboration and Innovation.

Alexander stepped back, the warmth of accomplishment washing over him. He looked at the team of creatures around him, their eyes sparkling with pride and satisfaction. They were not just a group of diverse creatures anymore; they were a team. A team that had learned to leverage their unique abilities, work together, innovate, and overcome a challenging task.

With a sense of awe, Alexander realized the power of collaboration and innovation. He had seen firsthand how seemingly insurmountable problems could be solved when a diverse team comes together, communicates effectively, and works towards a common goal. The monument was a testament to this. He felt a rush of admiration for the creatures around him and gratitude for Sage's wisdom.

Alexander looked up at the monument, then back at the creatures. "We did this. Together," he said, his voice ringing with pride and reverence. "Our differences, our unique abilities didn't set us apart. They brought us together. They made us...stronger."

The creatures seemed to understand, their sounds of affirmation filling the night air. At that moment, Alexander understood the true essence of collaboration and the transformative power of innovation.

He knew this understanding was a significant step in his journey, a lesson he would carry with him to NexGen Island and back to Stagnant Shores.

***

As the Valley's light began to fade, giving way to a sky filled with countless stars, Alexander found himself sitting atop a small hill overlooking the now thriving valley. He observed the Flutterers, Builders, and Tinkers, each performing their roles in harmonious synchronization, their individual skills combining to create a powerful force of collaboration and innovation.

This sight sparked a profound realization within Alexander. He had begun this journey with the creatures as disparate beings, each with their own skills and abilities. But through mutual understanding, respect, and collaboration, they had come together as an effective team. Their unity had not diluted their individuality; instead, it amplified their strengths, enabling them to achieve more than they could have alone.

The transformation was not just confined to the creatures, though. Alexander himself had evolved. He had learned to lead without dominating, to understand without assuming, and to respect without bias. The valley's challenge had been a test of his adaptability and understanding, and he felt he had emerged victorious, richer with experience and insight.

He leaned back, his gaze affixed on the star-studded sky. A gentle breeze rustled through the valley, carrying with it the murmurs of collaboration, the whispers of innovation. Alexander knew that this experience would forever be etched in his memory, a testament to the power of unity in diversity. He closed his eyes, his heart filled with a newfound respect for collaboration and innovation, his mind preparing for the next part of his journey.

***

As Alexander's thoughts began to settle, a new curiosity began to stir within him. It was as if the valley, sensing his readiness, was now revealing the next leg of his journey. To the east, the silhouettes of what seemed like a vast river snaking its way through the terrain began to manifest under the starlight. The water was calm, but even from this distance, Alexander could discern a subtle, captivating rhythm, like a distant whisper carried by the wind.

Sage's words returned to him then, "Beyond the valley, you will encounter the River of Storytelling, Alexander."

In that moment, the soft gurgling of the water seemed to morph into myriad voices, each narrating a tale, their notes rising and falling like a symphony of stories waiting to be heard, understood, and shared. It was clear that his next challenge was unlike any he had faced before.

Taking a deep breath, Alexander turned his gaze back to the bustling valley below. He would rest, recharge, and at dawn, he would embark on the new phase of his journey. He was ready to immerse himself in the world of stories, ready to navigate the River of Storytelling.

Chapter 6
The River of Storytelling

A gentle rustle in the wind heralded Alexander's arrival at the edge of the River of Storytelling. The sight that greeted him was nothing short of ethereal. The river was a tapestry of iridescent light, weaving and flowing in gentle undulations. It hummed with an unworldly resonance, sending a cascade of silvery melodies through the air.

Spellbound, Alexander reached out. His fingers skimmed the radiant surface, causing ripples of light to dance away from his touch, each one singing a different tale. The heroic exploits of legendary warriors, the heart-rending sorrows of lost lovers, the profound wisdom of ancient philosophers—all echoed in the river's voice, a grand symphony of narratives.

His heart beat in time with the river's lyrical whispers, matching the cadence of its ever-changing stories. The intoxicating allure of the river tugged at him, its radiant tales reaching out, beckoning him to listen, understand, and engage.

Bathed in the river's luminescence, Alexander felt a shiver of anticipation ripple through him. He knew he stood before a challenge that was more than just physical. The river held a test of empathy, comprehension, and connection—Alexander had to tap into the power of storytelling. As the mesmerizing dance of light and melody swirled around him, he took a deep breath, ready to dive into this new stage of his journey.

Listening to the countless stories whispered by the river, Alexander felt overwhelmed. It was a harmonious blend of countless narratives, each carrying a unique rhythm, a unique melody. As he listened, he found himself drawn into the stories, getting lost in their depth.

Just then, Sage's voice echoed in his mind, "Listen closely, Alexander. Each story, each narrative that the river shares carries a piece of wisdom. To navigate it, you must listen, understand and appreciate the power of storytelling."

"Alexander, remember that storytelling is not merely about weaving tales. It's about resonating with the listener, stirring their emotions, painting a picture with your words. It's about influence and inspiration. To steer your course through this river, you must resonate with its narratives."

Alexander, his hand still resting on the river's surface, nodded, his eyes filled with determination. "I understand, Sage. I will listen to the river's stories, understand their wisdom, and learn to appreciate the power of storytelling."

As he spoke, the river's whispers grew more intense, like it was responding to Alexander's resolve. Its surface rippled with a new fervor, reflecting the young man's determined gaze back at him. With this, Alexander understood that his journey through the River of Storytelling was about to begin.

As Alexander prepared himself to engage with the river's vast narratives, he once again heard Sage's voice in his mind. It was as if she was there with him, her wisdom guiding him in this crucial moment.

"Alexander," Sage began, her voice as steady as ever, "understanding the power of storytelling is crucial not just to navigate this river, but for your journey towards becoming a leader."

Alexander, with his ears tuned to Sage's voice, replied, "But Sage, I'm just trying to get to NexGen Island. How does storytelling tie into leadership?"

Sage, her voice resonating with wisdom, explained, "Storytelling, Alexander, is the soul of leadership. Leaders don't just give orders; they inspire, they influence. And to do that, they need to tell compelling stories that resonate with their followers. They need to paint a vivid picture of their vision that can drive others towards a common goal."

"Storytelling allows leaders to connect on a deeper emotional level, instilling a sense of purpose and direction. When a story is told well, it can move people to act, influence change, and drive progress. So, you see, Alexander, to lead the change you envision for Stagnant Shores, you must become a master storyteller."

Listening to Sage's insights, Alexander felt a shift within him. He looked at the murmuring river with renewed determination, ready to embrace the power of storytelling and its role in leadership.

***

Bathed in the golden light of the setting sun, Alexander stood by the river's edge, immersing himself in the river's rhythmic murmur. It was as if the river was a storyteller, and each ripple was part of an ongoing saga. But the words were shrouded in a language he struggled to comprehend.

"Speak to me, River," Alexander requested, his voice barely above a whisper.

The river responded, its flow intensifying. Yet the tales remained elusive, a symphony of sounds just beyond his understanding. His brow furrowed in concentration as he strained to decipher the river's language, but it was like trying to grasp water - the more he squeezed, the more it slipped away.

In his frustration, a memory of Sage surfaced. Her words resonated in his mind, "Stories, Alexander, aren't just about the words spoken or written. They're about the emotions they stir, the connections they forge. Listen not just with your ears, but with your heart."

With a renewed mindset, Alexander took a deep breath, calming his rushing thoughts. He listened again, not just for words but for feelings, connections, and experiences shared by the river. He let the river's whispers wash over him, seeping into his being.

As he surrendered to the rhythm of the river, the previously elusive words began to materialize. He started recognizing fragments of stories - tales of courage, resilience, triumph, and even loss. The realization of the power embedded in these narratives filled him with awe.

"No, I don't just hear you, River," Alexander finally responded, his voice echoing his newfound understanding and respect, "I comprehend your stories, and I'm prepared to share mine."

***

The night deepened, and the river's tales echoed in Alexander's ears. He sat by the river, his eyes closed, completely engrossed in the story of the mighty oak tree. As he listened, the words began to weave themselves into a coherent narrative. He felt an affinity with the oak tree, standing tall against the storms, bending but not breaking. It was a tale of resilience, adaptability, survival, exactly what Sage had taught him.

The river then asked, its voice a hushed whisper, "Alexander, do you have a story to share?"

Alexander drew a deep breath, "I do," he began, his voice filled with determination and passion, "It's a story of a man from a stagnant town. A man who dared to dream, dared to change. He ventured through the sea of knowledge, climbed mountains with modern tools, and learned the power of collaboration in a lively valley."

As Alexander narrated his journey, the river listened, its flow slowing as if hanging onto his words. As he concluded, the river shimmered under the moonlight, revealing a clear path across its depth. "Your story, Alexander, is a testament to your spirit," the river resonated, "You may cross."

At that moment, Alexander realized that storytelling was more than just a form of entertainment. It was a tool of influence, a way to build connections, even with a river. With newfound confidence, he stepped onto the illuminated path, acknowledging the power of storytelling and ready to face the next phase of his journey.

***

As Alexander stepped onto the riverbank, the water's voice fell silent, leaving an echo of tales in his mind. Each droplet rolling off his sodden clothes seemed to tell a story of its own, whispering the language of the river. The world around him buzzed with unspoken narratives; the rustling trees, the wind's murmur, the distant owl's hoot, all part of a larger story.

Suddenly, Alexander felt a presence, familiar and comforting. Sage's voice echoed in his mind, like a soft breeze, "Alexander, you've understood the soul of stories, now part of your essence."

"No longer are stories just tales for me, Sage," Alexander's voice rang out clear and steady in the twilight. "They are bridges, spanning hearts and minds, connecting souls. They hold the power to inspire, to lead, to transform."

A soft chuckle resonated in his mind, Sage's warm affirmation, "Indeed, Alexander. Stories are the most powerful tool we have for influence and change. They reflect who we are, and in turn, shape us. Remember this lesson as you continue your journey."

As the chuckle faded, the night grew still. Alexander felt a newfound sense of purpose. The journey ahead was long, and challenges awaited, but armed with the power of storytelling, he felt ready. Each tale he had deciphered in the river had led him closer to the person he was becoming, the leader he aspired to be. With newfound determination, he took a step forward, the power of narrative echoing in his heart, guiding him onwards.

***

As the final glimmers of the moon faded, surrendering to the gentle embrace of dawn, Alexander found himself standing at the threshold of a different challenge - The Winds of Adaptability. Rising in the distance, this vast expanse was known to be a place of constant change, of unpredictable gusts, of abrupt shifts from gentle breezes to tempests.

"Alexander," Sage's voice echoed in his memory, her words vivid as ever, "Adaptability is our greatest strength. Remember, life is never static; it's a relentless flux. And in the Winds, you'll face this truth.

But remember, it's not the strongest who survive, but those most responsive to change."

With Sage's advice resounding in his ears, Alexander stood tall, a slight shiver running down his spine as the cool morning breeze brushed against his skin. He felt the adrenaline rush, the thrill of anticipation prickling his senses. But there was also a flicker of apprehension, the fear of the unknown threatening to dampen his spirit.

Yet, as he looked back at the River of Storytelling, which now flowed quietly behind him, he remembered his journey - the hurdles he'd crossed, the lessons he'd learned. His eyes held the gleam of determination, his spirit fueled by the victories of his past.

The Winds of Adaptability loomed ahead, whispering tales of change, challenges, and evolution. Alexander, filled with resolve, squared his shoulders and looked towards the horizon. The dawn was breaking, and with it, a new chapter in his journey was about to unfold. His next test awaited him, ready to mould him, to test his mettle, to dance with him in the rhythm of change.

Chapter 7
The Winds of Adaptability

From the flat plains, a sense of anticipation grew, culminating in a tempest of turbulent winds - the Winds of Adaptability. Unlike any storm Alexander had ever encountered, these winds didn't follow a set pattern; they twisted and turned, ebbing and flowing with a disconcerting unpredictability.

They were a tangible reflection of the real world, mirroring its constant change and incessant flux. As the winds morphed, so too did the landscape, with cities transitioning into deserts, and forests reshaping into urban expanses, illustrating life's impermanence and the inevitable shifts in one's path.

Watching this spectacle of change, Alexander felt a knot of apprehension form in his gut. This was no mere physical challenge - it was a manifestation of life's unpredictability, a test of his ability to adapt. As he looked at the storm, he was reminded of Sage's words: "The only constant in life is change. Adaptability is your greatest asset." It was a lesson Alexander knew he'd have to remember if he was to navigate through the storm.

***

As the Winds of Adaptability began their wild dance, Alexander felt their force against his frame. It was a maelstrom of change, relentless and intimidating. He attempted to brace himself, digging his heels into the ground, hoping to resist the storm's fury.

"No use... too strong," he muttered, his voice barely audible over the howling gale. He pressed on, his knuckles white as he clung onto his walking staff, the wind whipping his cloak around him. He was like a stubborn tree trying to stand tall amidst a hurricane.

Suddenly, a gust of wind stronger than the others swept him off his feet. "No!" Alexander cried out, tumbling amidst the torrent of wind. He struggled to regain his footing, his face a picture of grit and determination.

Panting heavily, he stood still amidst the whirlwind, his eyes reflecting the harsh truth he'd been trying to avoid. "I can't... resist it," he gasped, the realization hitting him harder than any gust of wind. His resistance had only left him exhausted and disoriented.

As he stood there, chest heaving, he understood that he had to rethink his approach. The Winds of Adaptability, a perfect storm of change and unpredictability, continued to whirl around him, waiting to see how he would respond to their challenge.

***

With a fierce gust tossing him about like a leaf, Alexander barely heard the faint whisper of Sage in his ear. "Alexander," her voice seemed to cut through the turmoil, "you can't resist these winds. They symbolize change, the constant evolution of our world. You can't fight change, you must adapt."

"Adapt?" Alexander yelled over the roaring winds, his voice laden with disbelief. "These winds are tossing me around like a plaything! How am I supposed to adapt to this?"

There was a pause, then Sage's voice came again, a calm amidst the storm. "By observing, understanding, and flowing with the changes, Alexander. Stop viewing the winds as your adversary. Instead, see them as teachers. They're not here to hinder you, but to show you a different way of navigating."

Alexander was silent, taking in Sage's words. It sounded absurd, counterintuitive. But as another gust of wind buffeted him, he realized his current method was leading him nowhere. With a deep breath, he decided to trust Sage's wisdom.

"Alright, Sage. I will adapt. I will flow with the winds," Alexander declared. The winds howled in response, as if acknowledging his resolve. It was a daunting decision, filled with uncertainty, yet it was a step towards the essential lesson of adaptability that the Winds of Adaptability intended to teach him.

With each passing day, Alexander's understanding of the Winds of Adaptability grew. Instead of dreading their approach, he found himself anticipating their gusts, a tinge of excitement in his heart. He wasn't just surviving the winds anymore; he was learning to navigate them, to leverage their power to propel himself forward.

There were still moments of uncertainty, of fear even, but now they were overshadowed by an increased sense of control and resilience. The winds were no longer his enemy but a challenging partner, pushing him to adapt and evolve.

***

One evening, as a particularly powerful gust swept across him, Alexander found himself not panicking but steadying his stance, angling his body to allow the wind to flow around him, not against him. He had anticipated this gust; he was ready.

And just like that, he realized he was in harmony with the wind. A smile spread across his face. He had adapted. He had learned to dance with the unpredictable Winds of Adaptability.

Overwhelmed by his realization, he exclaimed into the roaring winds, "We are not at odds anymore! I've learned your rhythm, your unpredictability. I have adapted, and I will continue to do so."

As if understanding his proclamation, the winds let out a thunderous roar, sweeping around him in a gust that felt like an acknowledgment of his growth. Yes, the winds were change, and Alexander had not just survived them, he had thrived in them.

Underneath the diamond-studded sky, Alexander stood, his form still vibrating from the challenge he had overcome. The once furious winds had now dulled into a soothing lullaby, whispering tales of change into the twilight. He had wrestled with the tempest and emerged not just intact, but transformed.

His gaze traced the path he had carved through the mighty gales, his heart echoing with the pulsating rhythm of the winds. "You are as constant and inevitable as change itself," he spoke into the wind, his voice steady, "You raged and roared, yet within your chaos, I found an order."

In the swirling dance of the Winds of Adaptability, Alexander had discovered an echo of life's inherent uncertainty and change. He had learned to listen, to adapt, to ride the winds rather than resist them. A newfound respect kindled within him, not just for the force he had tamed, but for the resilience within himself that it had unearthed.

As the winds hummed their acknowledgement, Alexander's eyes twinkled with a new resolve. The boy who had entered the storm had now emerged a man molded by the wisdom of adaptability.

Drawing in a deep breath, he turned towards the unseen horizon, the silhouette of the upcoming challenges barely visible against the starlit sky. His heart pounded with a blend of exhilaration and anticipation as he stood on the precipice of another adventure. Change was inevitable, but so was his will to adapt and grow.

***

As the tempestuous dance of the Winds of Adaptability finally ceased, a sudden tranquility enveloped Alexander. The change was jarring yet serene, like the quiet that falls upon a battlefield after the storm of war. In the peaceful silence, a fragrant breeze, distinct and inviting, whispered to him, beckoning him forward.

His gaze fell upon the horizon, where the chaotic grey of the storm gave way to a lush spectacle. A garden, spread out like a patchwork quilt of vibrant colors, loomed in the distance. Each patch, he noticed, was distinct yet seamlessly blending with the others, creating an intriguing medley.

As he stood at the threshold of this new chapter, he recalled a cryptic piece of advice from Sage, "To create a symphony, Alexander, one needs many notes." The meaning of these words, unclear before, started to form a silhouette in his mind, mirroring the diverse patterns of the garden below.

With the storm behind him and the promise of another adventure twinkling in the garden ahead, Alexander moved forward. The tranquility of the scene stood in stark contrast to the challenge he knew awaited him. Yet, he stepped into the Garden of Diversity, his heart brimming with determination, ready to compose his symphony.

Chapter 8

The Garden of Diversity

After surviving the tumultuous Winds of Adaptability, Alexander found himself standing at the entrance of an entirely different challenge: The Garden of Diversity. This world was teeming with life, a stark contrast to the monotone landscapes he knew. As he approached the vibrant spectacle, memories of Sage's counsel filled his mind like whispers from another realm.

Underneath towering trees, their branches reaching out like the arms of ancient giants, delicate ferns played hide and seek. A canvas of flowers bloomed in every imaginable hue, their perfume saturating the air with an intoxicating sweetness. Amidst these blossoms, rugged cacti stood defiant, their spiky exteriors a testament to their resilience. The intertwining of fruit-bearing plants and creeping vines formed complex botanical mazes, while peculiar-looking fungi nestled in the cool, shadowed corners added an extra layer of intrigue.

Intrigued, Alexander turned to the compass, a powerful artifact bestowed upon him by Sage. "This is...unexpected. Unlike anything I've seen before. Back home, our fields, our forests...they're all so...predictable. This? It's a...a riot of life!"

The compass glowed faintly in response, and Sage's voice echoed from within its depths. "Yes, Alexander. This garden, with all its unexpected inhabitants, is a testament to the power of diversity. Every plant, every creature here, regardless of its form, adds something unique to this ecosystem. Just like how every person, regardless of their strengths and weaknesses, adds value to their community."

As Alexander digested Sage's words, he realized that this garden was more than just a beautiful spectacle. It was a living example of coexistence, of resilience born from diversity. It seemed like a complex tapestry where each thread, no matter how different, had a purpose and place. This thought left Alexander feeling both humbled and awestruck.

With the guidance of Sage's wisdom through the compass, Alexander gazed at the garden. This was a place where each entity, despite its shape, size, or color, contributed to a robust, resilient ecosystem. It was unlike anything he'd ever experienced. This garden, in all its diverse beauty, was a teacher – and Alexander was its eager student.

As he journeyed deeper into the garden, he encountered various creatures living in harmony with the flora, each playing a vital role in the balance of life. Butterflies flitted from flower to flower, pollinating as they went. Bees hummed a chorus of productivity, busily collecting nectar. The gentle rustle of leaves revealed the presence of small creatures finding refuge among the greenery.

Alexander was moved by the harmony of this ecosystem, and a sense of interconnectedness washed over him. He realized that just as every element in the garden had its purpose, every individual had a role to play in the greater tapestry of life.

Through the compass, Sage's voice offered guidance in this living lesson. "Embrace the beauty of diversity, Alexander, for it is the key to resilience and growth. Just as each plant and creature contributes to this garden's vitality, so too does every person contribute to the world's richness."

As the sun dipped below the horizon, painting the sky with hues of orange and pink, Alexander sat amidst the flourishing garden, feeling a profound sense of gratitude and wonder. This place had taught him that differences were not to be feared but celebrated, and that by recognizing the value of each unique individual, he could create a stronger, more harmonious world.

With a heart filled with newfound wisdom, Alexander knew that he would carry the teachings of the Garden of Diversity with him as he continued his journey. He understood that embracing diversity and appreciating the contributions of all would be his compass guiding him towards making a lasting impact in the world.

***

As Alexander began to explore the intricate ecosystem of the Garden of Diversity, he suddenly felt a gentle hand on his shoulder. Startled, he turned around to find Sage standing there, her eyes twinkling with warmth and wisdom.

"Sage, you're here!" Alexander exclaimed in astonishment.

"Yes, my dear Alexander," Sage replied with a serene smile. "I am here, not just in your memories or the compass, but physically present to guide you through this magnificent garden."

Alexander couldn't believe his eyes, yet there she was, standing beside him, her presence a comforting reassurance amidst the overwhelming beauty of the garden.

"This garden is stunning!" Alexander said, gesturing at the vibrant colors and patterns surrounding them.

"Indeed, Alexander, it is. And each plant, each creature you see here plays an essential role in maintaining the garden's vitality," Sage responded, pointing to a towering tree providing shade to a multitude of plants thriving in its shadows.

"Alexander, consider this tree. It's not just a structure; it's a habitat, a protector, a nurturer. It safeguards the soil from erosion, gives shelter to countless creatures, and offers shade to the plants below, enabling them to flourish."

As Alexander listened, he watched a vibrant parrot nestling on a tree branch. Following Alexander's gaze, Sage continued, "That parrot you're watching? It plays a vital role too, in seed dispersal. It's a gardener in its own right, shaping the garden's future by where it drops the seeds."

They strolled to a field of dazzling flowers, a flurry of bees dancing from one bloom to another. "Look at the bees and flowers, Alexander. They share a symbiotic relationship. The flowers provide nectar, which is food for the bees. In return, the bees help in pollination, allowing the flowers to reproduce. One cannot exist without the other."

Alexander's eyes widened in awe as he started to grasp the complex relationships and dependencies in the garden. He voiced his thoughts, "This is truly amazing, Sage. Every creature, every plant has a purpose and role here. They all contribute to maintaining balance."

Sage nodded, looking at Alexander with a satisfied smile. "Exactly, Alexander! And just like this garden, every person in a society, regardless of their role, contributes to its well-being and progress. Recognizing this is key to appreciating and promoting diversity."

Feeling a newfound connection with Sage, Alexander walked alongside her, observing the harmonious dance of life unfolding in the garden. With her guidance, he learned that diversity was not merely a concept but a living, breathing reality. It was about acknowledging the uniqueness of each individual and the strengths they brought to the table.

As they continued their journey through the garden, Alexander witnessed how every plant and creature coexisted in perfect harmony, each adding value to the other's existence. The garden taught him the significance of empathy, compassion, and collaboration, allowing him to envision a society where diversity was cherished and celebrated.

As the day waned, they sat under the shade of a magnificent tree, its branches a sanctuary for various creatures. Sage's presence was like a soothing balm to Alexander's soul, and he knew that her guidance would remain with him throughout his journey.

"Sage, thank you for being here with me," Alexander said with heartfelt gratitude.

"You are most welcome, Alexander," Sage replied with a serene smile. "Remember, the lessons you've learned here extend far beyond this garden. Carry them with you, and let them shape your decisions as you continue your adventure."

With the sun setting on the horizon, casting a golden glow over the Garden of Diversity, Alexander felt a sense of purpose and determination. The journey had taught him the importance of embracing diversity, nurturing resilience, and cherishing every contribution, no matter how big or small.

With Sage's wisdom etched in his heart, Alexander embarked on the next phase of his adventure, eager to make his mark on the world and create a future where diversity thrived and flourished. And with every step he took, he knew that he carried not just the compass, but the essence of Sage's teachings within him, guiding him through the challenges that lay ahead.

***

The morning sun had just started to spread its warmth when Sage approached Alexander, his eyes fixed on a particular cluster of plants in the garden. "Look, Alexander," she said, her voice slightly tinged with worry.

Alexander followed Sage's gaze. A certain group of plants, once vibrant with color and life, was now wilting, their leaves turning a sickly yellow. The sight was unsettling, a stark contrast to the thriving diversity around it.

"The garden has been struck by a disease," Sage explained, her gaze not leaving the dying plants.

Alexander felt a pang of alarm. "Is the entire garden in danger, Sage?" he asked, fearing the loss of the lush diversity he had grown to admire.

Sage, however, remained calm. "Patience, Alexander. Observe and learn," she advised.

In the days that followed, Alexander watched the disease's progression closely. It claimed a few more victims, yet it seemed to struggle to infiltrate the entire garden. Only certain types of plants fell victim, while others remained untouched. The infected ones wilted and returned to the soil, but their absence was quickly filled by other plants, those resilient to the disease.

***

One morning, about a week later, Alexander woke up to find the garden flourishing again, the disease's devastating effects almost erased.

Sage joined Alexander, a knowing smile on her face. "You see, Alexander," he began, "In a diverse system like our garden, a single threat might affect some, but it will rarely conquer all. Each plant species here has its unique strength, its unique resistance to different diseases. When one falls, another rises. That's the power of diversity. It breeds resilience."

Alexander absorbed Sage's words, a sense of awe washing over him. The garden had taught him an invaluable lesson, one that he would carry with him on his journey ahead. It was not just a garden, but a symbol of strength in diversity.

"Alexander, do you understand why the garden could recover so swiftly?" Sage asked, her gaze fixed on the sea of green around them.

Alexander paused, his eyes scanning the myriad of plants before him. They were so varied, yet harmonious, every species contributing its unique strength to the collective. "It's because of their diversity, isn't it, Sage?"

"Indeed, Alexander," Sage affirmed, a smile tugging at the corners of her mouth. "Each plant, each creature here possesses its unique strengths and weaknesses. Some plants resisted the disease that others could not withstand. When one fell, others stood strong. That's the essence of diversity."

"But that's not all," Sage continued, her voice echoing through the garden. "Diversity here does not merely end with resistance to diseases. It extends to how these plants adapt to varying conditions - dry, wet, cold, hot. Each one has carved out its niche where it thrives the best."

As Sage's words unfurled, Alexander looked at the garden with newfound admiration. Each plant, insect, even the micro-organisms in the soil, were threads interwoven into a resilient web. Their collective strength lay in their diversity, and that was the garden's true resilience against any single threat.

"I see," Alexander murmured, the lesson taking root in his mind. "A community's strength isn't in its uniformity but its diversity. Every unique trait contributes to its overall resilience."

Sage nodded approvingly. "Very well understood, Alexander. Always remember, diversity isn't about being different for the sake of difference. It's about leveraging those differences to build a robust and adaptable whole."

As Alexander meandered through the lush diversity of the garden, he paused at a seemingly discordant group of plants. Strikingly different in their colors, shapes, and sizes, they nonetheless existed harmoniously, each contributing to the overall vibrancy of the garden. The diversity he witnessed provoked a deeper thought.

"Alexander," Sage began, her voice reverberating through the colorful array, "This beautiful array of life you see, each plant distinct yet interdependent, is akin to our society. Do you see the connection?"

Alexander turned to Sage, his face knitted in contemplation. "Are you suggesting that our individualities, our unique skills, and backgrounds are like these diverse plants?"

Sage nodded, a gentle smile on her face. "Yes, exactly. Each one of us, with our unique abilities, experiences, and perspectives, contributes to the whole, just like each plant in this garden."

As Alexander looked around, Sage's words resonated with him. He had witnessed the opposite in the uniform landscapes where all plants were identical. There, a single disease could wreak havoc, and a change in conditions could lead to ruin. The analogy was clear now. "So, uniformity, or homogeneity, can lead to vulnerability," Alexander surmised.

"Correct, Alexander," Sage affirmed, pointing to the garden. "You see, in this garden, when a disease strikes, it may affect one kind of plant, but the others continue to thrive. It's the same with our society. Homogeneity might seem convenient in the short run, but in the face of a challenge or change, it exposes us to risk. Diversity, on the other hand, not only brings resilience but also fosters creativity and innovation."

A newfound understanding washed over Alexander. The interplay of different plants, their harmonious coexistence despite their differences, mirrored the diverse societies. And the strength that diversity conferred was evident - in the garden and beyond. This lesson was profound, reshaping his perspective on leadership and teamwork. Alexander looked at Sage, gratitude reflecting in his eyes, "Thank you, Sage. This is a lesson I will carry forward in my journey."

Alexander stood at the threshold of the Garden of Diversity, his heart echoing with the myriad lessons that this magical place had bestowed upon him. He drank in the riot of colors, the harmonious chaos of flora flourishing in all its glory. Each plant, distinct in its form, contributed to the flourishing garden, much like each unique individual who adds value to a community.

He turned to Sage, his eyes glistening with profound understanding. "I've been thinking about my journey, Sage. The Sea of Lifelong Learning taught me the importance of continuous growth. The Forest of Human Behavior illuminated the essence of emotional intelligence. The Mountains of Modern Tools revealed the power of leveraging technology. And this garden... it's opened my eyes to the strength that lies in diversity. All these places, they've transformed me."

Sage, listening attentively, nodded. "That's the power of embracing different experiences, Alexander. It changes your perspective, allows you to grow in ways you never thought possible."

Alexander nodded, a slow smile spreading across his face. "It's not just about acknowledging diversity, is it? It's about celebrating it, leveraging it. Without the variety of plants here, the garden wouldn't have survived the disease. In the same way, we need diverse minds and skills in our societies, in our teams, to tackle the complex challenges we face."

Sage smiled warmly. "Precisely, Alexander. In diversity, there is resilience, there is creativity, there is innovation. And above all, there is unity."

As Alexander took one last look at the Garden of Diversity, he felt a surge of gratitude. He had learned invaluable lessons, lessons that would guide him as a leader, as an individual. The vibrantly diverse landscape behind him served as a stark contrast to the uniformity he had known, a testament to the beautiful chaos that was life itself.

Sage clapped a hand on Alexander's shoulder, stirring him from his thoughts. "Are you ready, Alexander?"

With newfound confidence, Alexander nodded. "I am, Sage. It's time to move forward, to continue this journey."

As he stepped away from the Garden of Diversity and onto the next part of his path, Alexander felt anticipation flutter in his chest. He didn't know what lay ahead, but he was prepared to face it, fortified by the wisdom he had gained.

Through the misty horizon, the Path of Impact awaited, a new challenge, a new learning. And Alexander, transformed by his journey through the Garden of Diversity, was ready to embrace it.

***

As the lessons from the Garden of Diversity imprinted on his heart, Alexander cast a lingering gaze over the now familiar terrain. The spirit of the garden, a vibrant testament to unity in diversity, would remain with him always. But new lessons awaited him. He could feel the pull, the anticipation of fresh wisdom to be gleaned.

Looking ahead, a path opened up to them, winding into the distance. A hazy outline hinted at the challenges it held, concealing its true form. It was rugged, unforgiving, and it twisted and turned as far as his eyes could see, vanishing into the horizon.

"The Path of Impact," Sage announced, her voice laced with a sense of mystery, pointing towards the path. His eyes held the glitter of excitement, the anticipation of a new journey. "Remember Alexander, every step taken on this path leaves a footprint, a mark on the world. That's the impact you wield, but to do so, you must traverse this path."

Alexander studied the path in the distance, thoughts swirling in his mind, the gravity of Sage's words settling in his heart. "Impact," he murmured, the word tasted heavy yet empowering on his tongue. "It's about influencing change, isn't it, Sage?"

"Indeed, Alexander," Sage answered, a smile playing on her lips. "But remember, it's not only about influencing change. It's about the right kind of change, the kind that makes a difference. Are you ready for such a journey, Alexander?"

Feeling a sudden rush of courage, Alexander nodded, his eyes locked onto the mysterious path ahead. "I am ready, Sage. The Path of Impact... I want to see where it leads."

Sage clapped Alexander's shoulder in approval, her eyes gleaming with an almost parental pride. "Very well, Alexander. The Path of Impact waits for no one. Let's embark on our new adventure."

As the two figures merged with the sprawling twilight, a sense of anticipation hung heavy in the air. The Path of Impact lay ahead, the next challenge in Alexander's heroic quest. It was a path that promised to sculpt him, transform him further, and prepare him for the trials and triumphs that lay ahead.

The Garden of Diversity was behind them, its lessons carved into the annals of Alexander's memory, but the Path of Impact stretched ahead, an embodiment of the unknown. A new chapter was about to commence in Alexander's saga, offering further wisdom, understanding, and the prospect of genuine transformation. It was a path that promised to test Alexander's resilience, adaptability, and his new-found knowledge about the power of diversity and storytelling. The path that lay ahead was unchartered and held stories untold, but the promise of a new dawn, a fresh challenge, propelled Alexander forward into the embracing arms of the mysterious unknown.

Chapter 9
The Path of Impact

Alexander's steps quickened with anticipation as he approached the entrance of the Path of Impact. As he passed through the archway, he felt an inexplicable sense of reverence wash over him. The atmosphere was charged with a tangible energy, almost like an electric current that tingled through the air.

The path unfurled before him, a mesmerizing tapestry of footprints imprinted on the ground. Each step taken by previous travelers had left its mark, forming a mosaic of experiences and impact. Some footprints were bold and large, etched into the earth with a deep sense of purpose. Others were delicate, almost ethereal, hinting at the subtle yet meaningful actions of compassionate hearts.

"Welcome to the Path of Impact, Alexander," Sage's voice resonated gently. "This is where the stories of those who've come before converge, where the imprints of their lives continue to inspire."

Alexander gazed at the myriad of footprints, each representing a life, a moment, and a choice. He noticed some prints were slightly faded, their significance diminishing with time, while others were still fresh and vibrant, pulsating with energy and influence.

Amidst the sea of footprints, Alexander spotted a set that stood out, larger than the rest. They seemed to belong to a formidable traveler whose impact had left an indelible mark on the island. Curiosity stirred within him, and he turned to Sage, seeking guidance.

"What are these impressive footprints, Sage? They seem to carry immense weight," Alexander inquired, eager to understand the tales they held.

Sage nodded thoughtfully, "Ah, those are the footprints of a legendary islander named Elandra. She was a visionary leader who forged paths where none existed. Her courage and determination inspired others to follow in her footsteps, creating a legacy of progress and innovation."

Alexander marveled at the thought of Elandra's journey and the impact she had made. He traced her footprints with his eyes, feeling a sense of awe and admiration for someone who had made such a profound difference.

As he ventured further along the path, Alexander encountered footprints that radiated warmth and kindness. These prints belonged to ordinary islanders who had done extraordinary things through simple acts of compassion.

"Look here, Alexander," Sage pointed to a pair of smaller footprints intertwined with larger ones. "These footprints tell a heartwarming tale of a young islander named Kavi, who befriended a lost baby bird and nursed it back to health. Kavi's actions inspired a movement of caring for the island's wildlife, fostering a culture of environmental stewardship."

Alexander marveled at the diversity of stories he encountered. Each footprint told of resilience, generosity, innovation, and empathy, reflecting the different facets of the human spirit.

As he walked further, Alexander noticed footprints left by artisans, scientists, educators, and healers, each with their unique essence imprinted on the path. He saw how the collective impact of these diverse individuals had shaped the island's growth and progress.

The Path of Impact taught Alexander that every step, no matter how small, could create ripples of change and touch the lives of others. It was a poignant reminder that each person had the power to make a difference in their own way.

As he continued on the path, Alexander felt a profound sense of responsibility settling within him. He realized that the footprints he would leave behind on this journey would also become part of the island's mosaic, contributing to its ever-evolving story.

With newfound determination, Alexander resolved to tread the path with purpose and intention, ensuring that his own footprints would be etched with acts of kindness, inspiration, and positive change.

He smiled at Sage, grateful for the profound lesson he had learned. "I now understand, Sage. The Path of Impact is a testament to the potential within each of us to leave a mark on the world. I am ready to make my own impact on NexGen Island."

With a curious glint in his eyes, Alexander turned to Sage, eager to uncover the secrets hidden within the footprints that adorned the Path of Impact. "What do these footprints truly signify, Sage? They seem to bear tales of triumph and wonder," he inquired, seeking to unravel the mysteries before him.

Sage smiled, the wisdom of ages reflecting in her eyes. "Each footprint you see etched on this path is a tangible record of impact," she began, his voice carrying the weight of generations past. "They represent the actions and choices of travelers who walked the same path as you do now."

Alexander's eyes widened, comprehending the profound implications of Sage's words. "Every step we take leaves a mark—a mark that tells a story," she whispered in awe.

"Indeed," Sage affirmed. "Some footprints reflect great strides, bold endeavors that forever altered the course of this island's history. Others may appear modest, yet their significance lies in the ripples of change they set in motion."

***

As they strolled along the path, Alexander keenly observed the array of footprints that surrounded him. He noticed the grand imprints left by visionaries and pioneers—those who dared to challenge the status quo and blaze new trails. Their footprints were deep, and their impact resonated through time.

"Those massive footprints over there," Sage pointed, "belong to a revered architect named Arion. He envisioned the first grand library on NexGen Island, a sanctuary of knowledge that has since enriched countless lives."

Alexander marveled at the size of Arion's footprints, symbolizing the vastness of his vision and the enduring legacy he left behind. "His impact is immeasurable," Alexander mused, "a testament to the power of a single idea."

Sage nodded, acknowledging Alexander's insight. "Indeed, one idea, one choice, can change the trajectory of generations to come."

As they continued along the path, Alexander noticed the footprints of everyday islanders—acts of kindness, compassion, and generosity imprinted gently on the earth.

"Look here," Sage said, gesturing towards a set of smaller footprints intermingled with larger ones. "These prints belong to a young girl named Elara. She planted a sapling in this very spot, and now, it stands tall, providing shade and sustenance for many."

Alexander smiled, understanding the significance of Elara's act. "Her small footprint made a big difference," he remarked. "It shows that every act of goodness counts."

"Indeed," Sage replied, her eyes shining with pride for the island's inhabitants. "The impact is not confined to grand gestures; even the tiniest footprints carry immense significance."

As they journeyed further, Alexander saw footprints representing various trades and professions—the artisans, scientists, healers, and educators—all contributing to the island's thriving community.

"These footprints weave a tapestry of diversity and knowledge," Sage explained. "They are a testament to the strength of a united community, each individual playing their part in shaping a better future."

Alexander nodded, humbled by the interconnectedness of all the footprints he witnessed. "They tell a story of unity and shared purpose," he observed.

"Yes," Sage replied, her voice gentle and wise. "Each step taken with purpose and empathy has the power to ignite change. Every footprint on this path holds a lesson, a reminder that our actions echo through time."

Alexander walked onward, his heart alight with the realization that his journey on the Path of Impact would be more than a mere stroll—it would be a conscious effort to create footprints of compassion, inspiration, and positive change. He knew that his actions, no matter how small, could make a difference, just like the countless travelers before him. And with this newfound understanding, he vowed to leave his own mark on NexGen Island, ensuring that his footprints would tell a story of love, hope, and impact for generations to come.

***

As Alexander continued his journey along the Path of Impact, he became enthralled by the vibrant tapestry of life that surrounded him. The footprints etched on the path were as diverse as the inhabitants of NexGen Island themselves, each telling a unique story of purpose and passion.

He spotted a group of musicians huddled together, their melodies blending harmoniously. Their footprints seemed to dance beside the notes, leaving behind an ethereal trail of artistry and joy. The music reached his ears, and he found himself swaying to the rhythm, captivated by the unity of their purpose.

Next, he came across a cluster of artisans, their hands diligently crafting intricate sculptures and artworks. Their footprints bore the mark of creativity and devotion, a testament to their commitment to preserving the island's rich artistic heritage.

As he moved on, Alexander spotted a healer tending to the sick, her footprints gentle and deliberate, reflecting the care and empathy she bestowed upon her patients. Her presence radiated warmth, and he couldn't help but be moved by the profound impact she had on the lives she touched.

Further along, he encountered a teacher surrounded by a group of eager young minds. Their footprints, though small, symbolized the knowledge and wisdom they gained through their shared journey of learning and growth. Alexander watched as the teacher's passion ignited the sparks of curiosity in the children's eyes, leaving a trail of inspiration in their wake.

In another corner of the path, he witnessed a group of environmentalists tirelessly planting trees and restoring the land. Their footprints embraced the earth, a testament to their dedication to preserving the island's natural beauty for future generations.

As the day progressed, Alexander encountered countless more footprints, each representing a story of impact—acts of kindness, entrepreneurship, community service, and innovation. He observed a farmer's footprints that sowed seeds of sustenance and abundance, a scientist's footprints leading to discoveries that pushed the boundaries of knowledge, and an inventor's footprints marking a path of ingenious creations that improved lives.

Amidst the diversity of footprints, Alexander began to notice a common thread—a shared commitment to making a positive difference. Everyone on NexGen Island, regardless of their role or profession, played a vital part in the community's collective journey towards progress and betterment.

Moved by the inspiring scenes unfolding before him, Alexander felt a sense of interconnectedness with the island's inhabitants. He realized that his own journey was interwoven with theirs, and that every step he took was an opportunity to leave an impact, no matter how big or small.

As the sun dipped below the horizon, casting a warm glow on the footprints before him, Alexander felt a renewed sense of purpose. He knew that his time on NexGen Island was not merely a passing visit, but a chance to contribute to its thriving community and leave a mark of positivity.

With newfound determination, he continued walking along the Path of Impact, eager to create footprints of his own. He was ready to embrace the diversity of experiences and lessons that lay ahead, knowing that each step he took would add to the symphony of footprints on this path of change and inspiration.

As the stars illuminated the night sky, Alexander whispered to himself, "Each footprint holds a story of impact, and I shall ensure that mine will be a tale of compassion, innovation, and purpose." With Sage's words echoing in his heart, he knew that the journey towards making a difference had only just begun, and he embraced it with unwavering resolve.

***

As the sun peaked above the horizon, Alexander awakened early to continue his trek along the Path of Impact. He couldn't shake off the thought of the footprints he had encountered earlier—the ones that symbolized true change and positive impact. The more he walked, the clearer it became: the path wasn't just a physical trail; it was a journey that transcended time, guided by purpose and the desire to make a lasting difference.

He found himself lost in introspection, retracing the steps of his past experiences. The memories of the Island of Expediency flooded his mind—the place where instant gratification had been glorified, and immediate gains were sought without a second thought. Back then, it had seemed exhilarating to achieve quick results, but as he delved deeper into the meaning of impact, he realized the shallowness of such pursuits.

Deep in thought, Alexander came across a group of travelers who were engaged in a spirited discussion about the importance of sustainable practices and long-term planning. The realization dawned on him that their focus was not on momentary triumphs, but on the collective well-being of the island and its inhabitants. Their footprints told stories of collaboration, innovation, and a commitment to leaving a legacy of change.

Curiosity getting the better of him, Alexander joined the conversation. "I've been on an expedition, seeking instant success and immediate rewards," he admitted, "but the footprints on this path tell a different story—a story of patient perseverance and purposeful action."

One of the travelers, a seasoned mentor with kind eyes, smiled warmly. "Ah, young traveler, you've taken the first step in understanding the essence of impact. The world may entice you with the allure of quick wins, but true change arises from a mindset that embraces the long-term effects of our choices."

As they talked, Alexander learned that the impact-oriented mindset was not just about the destination; it was about the journey and the transformative power of the process. It involved assessing the consequences of actions on individuals, communities, and the environment, and choosing a course that nurtured growth and sustainable progress.

Another traveler chimed in, "We mustn't lose sight of the bigger picture. Impact isn't always loud and flashy; it can be gentle and gradual, like the blooming of a flower. It's the small acts of kindness and compassion that ripple outward, creating waves of positive change."

Alexander nodded, absorbing their words. He thought back to the Garden of Diversity, where he had witnessed the strength of a community of diverse flora, each plant playing its role in maintaining the garden's resilience. Diversity, he realized, was another aspect of impact—an acknowledgment that different perspectives and strengths were necessary to create a thriving ecosystem.

As he bid farewell to the travelers and continued on the path, Alexander couldn't help but feel a sense of purpose rising within him. The desire to create a positive impact, no matter how big or small, burned brightly in his heart.

He recalled Sage's stories about past travelers who had left their mark on the world—leaders who had inspired generations, innovators who had transformed industries, and artists whose creations had touched souls. The footprints on the path were not just marks on the ground; they were a testament to the power of intention and action.

In the midst of this realization, Alexander also recognized the limitations of a short-sighted mindset—one that focused solely on immediate gains without considering the long-term consequences. He understood that a myopic view could lead to unintended negative outcomes and hinder progress toward creating a better world for future generations.

With each step, Alexander's sense of responsibility deepened. He knew that the choices he made and the impact he left behind would shape the legacy he left on NexGen Island. And so, he pledged to walk the Path of Impact with integrity and compassion, driven by the belief that every action, no matter how small, had the potential to create a ripple of positive change.

As the sun set on the horizon, casting a golden glow over the footprints once more, Alexander felt a profound sense of purpose and a renewed determination to make his mark on the world. The journey ahead was filled with uncertainties, but he knew that with an impact-oriented mindset, he had the power to leave a lasting impression on the hearts of those he encountered and the world he inhabited.

With every step, he whispered to himself, "I shall walk this path with the knowledge that my actions have the potential to shape destinies and touch lives. I shall embrace the impact-oriented mindset and let it guide me to create a better, more compassionate world."

And so, with Sage's teachings resonating in his heart, Alexander continued his expedition along the Path of Impact—a journey fueled by purpose, driven by compassion, and destined to leave a legacy of positive change.

***

As Alexander stood amidst the footprints on the Path of Impact, he felt a surge of emotions wash over him. The journey had been nothing short of extraordinary, and the lessons he had learned along the way had left an indelible mark on his heart.

"I never imagined how powerful diversity could be," Alexander said, turning to Sage. "In the Garden of Diversity, I saw how each plant contributed uniquely to the ecosystem's vitality. It made me realize that embracing differences is the key to a thriving community."

Sage smiled, nodding in agreement. "Indeed, my young traveler. Diversity is like the colors of a vibrant painting, each hue adding depth and beauty. It enriches us, making us stronger and more resilient."

As they continued down the path, Alexander observed the footprints left by inhabitants of NexGen Island. Some were big, others small; some had been etched deeply into the ground, while others were lighter, barely visible. Each represented an act of impact, and Alexander couldn't help but marvel at the variety of ways people had left their mark.

"I used to think that making an impact had to be grand, like changing the world overnight," Alexander admitted. "But these footprints show that impact can take many forms, big or small, and that every action counts."

"Exactly," Sage affirmed. "Every step matters, for even the tiniest pebble creates ripples in the water. Impact is not always immediate or visible, but its effects can be profound."

As they ventured further, Alexander noticed a footprint that seemed slightly faded. "What about those whose impact seems to diminish over time? What if they are forgotten?" he wondered.

Sage paused, considering Alexander's question thoughtfully. "Sometimes, the truest impact lies in the lives we touch and the memories we leave behind. Even if footprints fade, the essence of our actions lives on in the hearts of those we've impacted."

Alexander took a moment to absorb Sage's wisdom. He realized that the journey of impact was not about seeking recognition or accolades, but about leaving behind a legacy of positivity and inspiration.

With every step, he became more aware of the shortcomings of focusing solely on immediate gains. "I used to think success was measured by wealth or achievements," Alexander confessed. "But true success lies in the positive change we bring to the world."

Sage smiled warmly. "You've grasped the heart of the matter, my dear traveler. Impact is not about personal gain; it's about enriching the lives of others and leaving the world a better place."

As they continued down the path, Alexander felt a sense of clarity he had never known before. He understood that his journey was not just about reaching a destination but about making a difference every step of the way.

The sun began to set, casting a golden glow over the footprints ahead. Each print was a testament to the power of humanity—the capacity to love, to heal, to inspire.

"I am grateful for this journey," Alexander said, his voice filled with reverence. "It has opened my eyes and heart to the true meaning of impact."

Sage placed a reassuring hand on his shoulder. "And your journey has only just begun, dear Alexander. The world is vast, and there are countless paths to explore. With an impact-oriented mindset, you will continue to create ripples of change wherever you go."

Alexander smiled, feeling a renewed sense of purpose. He knew that the Path of Impact was not just a physical trail; it was a mindset, a way of living and embracing the diversity and potential within himself and others.

With every passing moment, he felt more determined to leave behind a legacy of positivity, compassion, and hope. As the stars emerged in the night sky, Alexander knew that the journey ahead held even greater wonders, and he was ready to make his mark on the world in the most profound and meaningful ways.

***

As Alexander stood at the crossroads of the Path of Impact, a faint rumble echoed in the distance. Sage turned to him with a knowing look in his eyes.

"My young friend, the next leg of your journey lies ahead—the Volcano of Failure," Sage said, her voice tinged with a mix of seriousness and anticipation.

Alexander's heart skipped a beat at the mention of the ominous-sounding challenge. "The Volcano of Failure? What awaits me there?" he asked, his curiosity piqued.

"It is a place where one must confront their fears, face setbacks, and embrace vulnerability," Sage explained. "In the heart of the volcano, you will find the crucible of growth and resilience."

Alexander swallowed hard, his mind flooded with doubts and uncertainties. Failure was a daunting prospect, and he couldn't help but wonder if he was ready to face it head-on.

"You may stumble, and you may fall," Sage continued, "but remember that failure is not the end—it is a catalyst for growth and an opportunity to rise stronger than before."

Despite the trepidation, Alexander knew he couldn't turn away from this challenge. The journey had taught him the value of adaptability, collaboration, and impact, and he understood that facing failure was an essential part of the adventure.

As they made their way toward the looming volcano, Alexander felt a mix of apprehension and determination. He knew that this next chapter in his journey would push him to his limits, testing his courage and resilience.

"The Volcano of Failure will reveal your inner strength," Sage said, her voice steady. "Embrace the lessons it offers, and you will emerge wiser and more resilient than ever before."

With those words, Alexander took a deep breath, steeling himself for the trials that lay ahead. The path might be treacherous, but he was no longer the hesitant traveler who began this journey. He had grown and evolved, and he was ready to face whatever challenges the Volcano of Failure had in store.

As they reached the edge of the volcano, Alexander cast one last look at the horizon, where the sun was setting in a blaze of colors. It was a reminder that even in the face of darkness and uncertainty, there was always the promise of a new day and the chance to rise again.

With a determined glint in his eye, Alexander stepped into the shadows of the volcano, ready to confront his fears and embrace the power of resilience. The adventure continued, and he knew that no matter the outcome, he was on a journey that would forever shape his soul and leave an impact on the world around him.

Little did he know that the Volcano of Failure would be the crucible that forged his truest self—a person unafraid to stumble, learn, and rise again, and in doing so, become an inspiration to others on their own paths of discovery and growth. The stage was set for Alexander's most transformative chapter yet, and the world awaited the tale of the young traveler who would face the fires of failure and emerge as a beacon of hope and possibility.

Chapter 10
The Volcano of Failure

Throughout his journey on the Path of Impact, Alexander experienced a transformation of the heart and mind. He had come to realize the immense importance of making a meaningful impact on the world around him. Each step he took, each decision he made, had the potential to create ripples that could touch the lives of others in profound ways.

Alexander's encounters with diverse individuals during his travels had shown him the power of collaboration and the strength that came from embracing differences. He learned that a united team with a common purpose could achieve far greater heights than any individual could alone. The stories Sage shared with him about past travelers who had left a lasting impact on the world inspired him to follow in their footsteps.

His time in the Garden of Diversity had opened his eyes to the beauty of individuality and the strength that stemmed from embracing a wide array of talents and perspectives. Each plant in the garden contributed uniquely to its vitality, and Alexander saw how this mirrored the potential of diverse teams and communities.

The AI-powered map in the Mountains of Modern Tools had taught him the value of leveraging technology for problem-solving. He realized that with the right tools and knowledge, one could overcome seemingly insurmountable obstacles.

Alexander's journey through the Valley of Collaboration and Innovation had been a masterclass in teamwork and creativity. The creatures he met represented different skillsets, and he saw how they came together to tackle challenges with unparalleled efficiency.

As he scaled the Mountains of Modern Tools, he came to understand the transformative power of modern technology when used correctly. The AI map had served as an essential guide, unlocking the potential of his journey.

His experience with the Winds of Adaptability had taught him the importance of embracing change and being adaptable. Like the trees in the Valley of Collaboration and Innovation, his ability to bend and adjust in the face of adversity determined his survival.

Throughout his adventures, Alexander had learned that an impact-oriented mindset wasn't about seeking recognition or immediate gains. It was about using one's unique skills and experiences to make a difference, no matter how big or small. Each step on his journey had brought him closer to understanding that the key to making a lasting impact was through empathy, collaboration, and embracing failure as a steppingstone to growth.

As Alexander stood at the base of the Volcano of Failure, he felt a sense of purpose burn within him. He knew that this next challenge would be a true test of his determination and resilience. The lessons he had learned so far had prepared him for this moment, and he was ready to face whatever trials lay ahead.

With Sage's guidance and the wisdom he had gained on his journey, Alexander was determined to climb the Volcano of Failure and emerge stronger on the other side. He understood that failure was not something to be feared but embraced as a vital part of the path to success.

As he took his first step towards the fiery ascent, Alexander reflected on the impact he wanted to leave on the world. He knew that the footprints he left behind would tell a story of growth, determination, and the unwavering belief in the power of making a difference. And with that, he began his ascent, ready to face the challenges of the Volcano of Failure with courage and resolve.

***

Alexander's heart pounded in his chest as he approached the base of the Volcano of Failure. The sight of the looming volcano stirred fear and apprehension within him. He couldn't help but feel overwhelmed by the magnitude of the challenge that lay ahead.

Sage noticed Alexander's unease and placed a reassuring hand on his shoulder. "The path ahead may seem daunting but remember that it is through facing our fears that we grow and learn," Sage said. "Failure is not the end; it is an opportunity for growth."

With Sage's words echoing in his mind, Alexander took a deep breath and began his ascent up the steep slopes of the volcano. The ground beneath his feet felt unsteady, as if every step he took could lead to a fall into the fiery abyss below. Fear gnawed at his heart, and doubt threatened to consume his determination.

"I can do this," he whispered to himself, trying to muster the confidence to press on. "I can overcome this fear."

As he climbed higher, the heat intensified, and the air grew thick with tension. Alexander's heart pounded loudly in his chest, matching the rhythm of his labored breathing. With each step, he felt the weight of the challenge ahead, the fear of failure lurking like a shadow at his side.

"Why am I even doing this?" he muttered, his voice barely audible over the rumbling of the volcano. "What if I'm not strong enough to face these challenges?"

Sage turned to him with a gentle smile. "Fear is a natural part of any journey," she said, her voice steady and reassuring. "It's okay to feel afraid, but remember that you are not alone in this ascent. I am here with you, and I believe in your strength and determination."

Alexander nodded, taking comfort in Sage's words. He knew that he couldn't let fear paralyze him. The path to making an impact was never meant to be easy, and he had to confront his fears head-on if he wanted to grow and succeed.

As they climbed higher, Alexander's legs grew weary, and his hands trembled with exhaustion. The heat from the lava below seemed to seep into his very bones, intensifying the struggle. But he refused to give in to the fear of failure. Each step he took was a testament to his determination to keep moving forward.

At times, the path grew narrow, and Alexander had to navigate through treacherous rocks and crevices. Doubt tried to infiltrate his thoughts, telling him that he might stumble and fall. Yet, he persisted, drawing strength from Sage's unwavering belief in him.

With each upward step, the fear of failing slowly gave way to a sense of purpose and resilience. Alexander began to realize that failure was not something to avoid at all costs but an inevitable part of any meaningful journey. It was through failure that he would learn and grow, gaining the experience and wisdom needed to make a lasting impact.

Finally, after what felt like an eternity of struggle, Alexander and Sage reached the summit of the Volcano of Failure. The view from the top was breathtaking, as if the entire world lay before them. The journey had been arduous, but the lessons learned along the way were priceless.

With a sense of accomplishment, Alexander looked back at the path he had taken, recognizing that each step, no matter how difficult, had been essential to his growth. The fear of failure still lingered, but it no longer controlled him. Instead, it fueled his determination to face whatever challenges lay ahead on the path of impact.

The wind whistled a solemn tune as Alexander and Sage stood shoulder to shoulder on the summit, the molten heart of the volcano beneath them. In the fiery glow, Alexander found an unusual sense of warmth, the lessons of failure fortifying his will. Sage's words had illuminated his path, casting aside the shadows of his doubts. He now viewed failure not as a devastating end but as the birthplace of resilience and strength.

"Are you ready, Alexander?" Sage asked, her voice echoing amidst the volcanic rumbles.

"Yes," he replied, his voice steady, his heart beating in sync with the rhythm of the volcano. He felt an inexplicable bond with this volatile entity, a shared kinship shaped by their dance with failure.

As the winds of change began to stir, Alexander turned to share another word with Sage. But to his shock, she was gone. The place where she had been standing was now empty. The moonlight cast an eerie shadow where she had once been. His mentor, his guide, was no longer beside him.

A shiver ran down his spine as bewilderment washed over him. His heart pounded in his chest like a drum, and his eyes darted around the volcano's summit, seeking his vanished mentor. "Sage?" he called out into the wind, but his voice was swallowed by the wind's howling and the volcano's ominous grumble.

Alone on the volcano's summit, Alexander felt a jolt of fear. His initial instinct was to panic, to call out again, but he quelled that urge. He drew in a deep breath, remembering Sage's wisdom, her emphasis on resilience, and the strength born from failure.

He was alone, yes, but he was not unprepared. He carried within him the potent lessons learned from each challenge on his journey so far, especially the Volcano of Failure. Alexander understood now that his journey was about transformation, resilience, and the courage to face whatever lay ahead.

The journey ahead was uncertain, fraught with unknown challenges and untold obstacles, yet Alexander was not afraid. Sage might have vanished, but she had left him armed with the knowledge to navigate his path. The wisdom she imparted was now a part of him, lighting his way in the darkest times.

As he stood alone on the volcano, his heart throbbed with renewed determination. He was prepared to carve his path, face whatever came his way, and ultimately make a lasting impact in his community. His journey was far from over, yet he felt ready to continue, ready to embrace the lessons that lay ahead. And so, with the spirit of Sage within him and the lessons of the Volcano of Failure as his beacon, Alexander stepped forth into the unknown, ready to embrace his destiny.

***

As Alexander steeled himself for the approaching trial atop the Volcano of Failure, an unexpected sound echoed through the air. It was a deep, throaty rumble, like the growl of a monstrous beast awakening from slumber. The very earth under Alexander's feet shivered, matching the tremors of anticipation running through his own heart. His eyes instinctively darted towards the volcano's heart.

Suddenly, the volcano gave a shuddering sigh and spewed forth a magnificent display of molten lava. It burst from the crater, a fiery geyser punctuating the otherwise quiet night. Sparks crackled in the heated air, mixing with the swirling ash, creating a stunning, albeit ominous spectacle.

The volatile demonstration was a stark reminder of the very essence of the Volcano of Failure. Its explosive force mirrored the inevitable missteps and stumbles everyone encounters in the journey of life. Each spark was like a setback, a mistake, a failure; each one a lesson waiting to be learned. It was a symbol of life's trials, relentless and sometimes unexpected, yet instrumental in molding resilience and strength.

Fear gripped Alexander's heart as he watched the eruption. The sight reminded him of his own fear of failure and the uncertainties that lay ahead. He felt a twinge of doubt, wondering if he was truly capable of making a lasting impact, considering the risks and challenges that came with it.

As if sensing Alexander's internal struggle, Sage's voice echoed within his mind. "Look closely, Alexander. This eruption may symbolize failure, but it also represents the growth that comes from it."

Alexander turned his attention back to the volcano, trying to understand Sage's words. As the lava flowed down the slopes, it left behind a trail of destruction, scorching the earth. Yet, he noticed something remarkable amid the devastation—the lava, as destructive as it seemed, also brought nourishment to the soil. The richness of the volcanic ash would eventually lead to new life and growth.

"Failure is not the end," Sage's voice continued to resonate from within his thoughts, "but a transformative process that prepares us for greater challenges and achievements. It's through failure that we gain experience, resilience, and the wisdom needed to overcome future obstacles."

Alexander pondered Sage's wisdom; his gaze fixed on the molten flow. He realized that failure was not something to fear but a stepping-stone towards growth and learning. Just like the volcano's eruption, failure could be harnessed as a force for positive change.

As the eruption subsided, Alexander felt a shift within himself. The fear of failure that once paralyzed him now felt like a mere obstacle to be conquered. He understood that his journey on the path of impact would be filled with ups and downs, but each challenge was an opportunity for growth and self-discovery.

With renewed determination, Alexander remembered Sage's advice from their earlier conversations. "Failure is not the end; it's a chance to learn and become better. I won't let fear hold me back anymore."

Though Sage wasn't physically present, her words continued to guide Alexander. He felt her wisdom and support in his heart as he stood atop the volcano, ready to face the eruptions and challenges that lay ahead.

With each step down the volcano, Alexander felt the weight of fear lifting from his shoulders. He knew that he had Sage's guidance and the valuable lessons from the Volcano of Failure to carry him through any future setbacks. As he walked, he remembered her saying, "Embrace failure as a part of your journey and use it to fuel your determination. Remember, it's okay to stumble, as long as you get back up and keep moving forward."

And so, with Sage's wisdom etched in his heart, Alexander continued his journey, his spirit unshaken by the possibility of failure. The path of impact lay ahead, filled with challenges and uncertainties, but he was now armed with the knowledge that failure was not the end of the road. It was merely a steppingstone towards a future filled with growth, resilience, and the potential to make a difference in the world.

***

As Alexander continued to stand at the base of the Volcano of Failure, his eyes scanned the vast landscape. The journey had been arduous, filled with obstacles and moments of self-doubt, but he had finally reached the summit. The distant memories of his early days on NexGen Island flooded his mind, reminding him of the lessons learned and the growth he had experienced.

With Sage's teachings echoing in his heart, Alexander felt a newfound sense of resilience and determination. He understood that failure was not the end but a steppingstone towards growth and progress. Each eruption of the volcano had symbolized moments of setbacks and mistakes, but they had also become opportunities for learning and improvement.

As he breathed in the crisp mountain air, Alexander thought back to the words of wisdom that Sage had shared with him during their time together. "Failure is a part of every journey, Alexander," she had said. "It is not something to be feared or avoided, but rather embraced. It is through failure that we learn, evolve, and ultimately succeed."

The memory of Sage's gentle smile and encouraging voice filled him with confidence. Alexander knew that he had changed during his travels, not just in his skills and abilities, but in his mindset. He now understood that success was not measured solely by achieving a goal but by the lessons learned along the way.

With a deep sense of gratitude, Alexander bowed his head in a silent moment of reflection. He was thankful for the challenges he had faced, for they had forged him into a more resilient and adaptable individual.

***

As Alexander began his trek away from the Volcano of Failure, he felt a mix of emotions swirling within him. He was eager to see what the next phase of his journey held, yet a touch of nostalgia lingered as he thought about leaving NexGen Island behind.

As he made his way back to the heart of the island, the people he had encountered during his adventure greeted him warmly. Their smiles and words of encouragement filled him with a sense of belonging. It was evident that he had made an impact on their lives, just as they had made an impact on his.

In the center of the island, Alexander found himself drawn to the tranquil spot where he had met Sage. The wise mentor sat there, her eyes twinkling with pride and wisdom.

"You've come a long way, Alexander," Sage said, her voice warm and soothing. "I see the growth in you, the resilience that has taken root in your heart."

Alexander nodded, grateful for the guidance Sage had provided throughout his journey. "I couldn't have done it without your wisdom, Sage. You taught me the importance of embracing failure and learning from it."

Sage smiled. "Indeed, failure is not the end, but the beginning of a new understanding. You now carry the knowledge of how setbacks can pave the way for greatness."

"I've come to realize that success is not just about reaching a destination," Alexander said thoughtfully. "It's about the impact we leave behind, the positive change we bring to the world."

"That's right, Alexander," Sage replied. "Your journey on NexGen Island was a microcosm of life's greater tapestry. Every experience, every person you encountered, contributed to the person you have become."

Alexander looked out at the island, cherishing the memories he had created and the connections he had forged. "I will carry the spirit of NexGen Island with me always," he vowed.

As the sun set on the horizon, Sage placed a hand on Alexander's shoulder. "Your journey does not end here, my dear. The path you now walk is a continuation of the impact you will make."

With a deep sense of purpose, Alexander bid farewell to the island and its inhabitants, knowing that he would always carry a piece of NexGen with him. As he sailed away, he felt a surge of determination to make a positive impact in every phase of his life, to leave footprints of change wherever he went.

And so, with the wisdom of Sage in his heart and the lessons of NexGen Island etched into his soul, Alexander set sail for new adventures, knowing that his journey was far from over. The next phase awaited him, and with it, the promise of continued growth, learning, and impact.

Chapter 11
The Return

As Alexander stood on the bow of his boat, he couldn't help but reflect on the lessons he had learned along the way. From the moment he set foot on NexGen Island, each chapter of his journey had been an enlightening revelation.

His voyage began with excitement and fear as he left his known world behind to uncover the secrets of the island. The sea of lifelong learning taught him the value of continuous knowledge acquisition, guided by his mentor Sage. The forest of human behavior tested his emotional intelligence, helping him interpret the behavior of the creatures he encountered. The mountains of modern tools introduced him to the transformative power of technology, empowering him to overcome challenges.

In the valley of collaboration and innovation, he learned the true strength of unity and the power of diversity. The river of storytelling imparted the art of connection and the timeless wisdom of narratives. The winds of adaptability demonstrated the necessity of adjusting his sails to embrace change and thrive.

In the lush Garden of Diversity, he understood the beauty and resilience that emerges from embracing differences. On the Path of Impact, he learned the importance of making a positive difference in the world and leaving a lasting imprint.

But it was the Volcano of Failure that left the most profound impression on Alexander. As he climbed the treacherous slopes and faced the eruptions of past failures, he grasped the transformative power of failing and trying again. Sage's counsel resonated within him, assuring him that growth emerges from the ashes of failure, igniting an unyielding determination to embrace failure as a steppingstone towards success.

With each lesson, Alexander's perspective expanded, his wisdom deepened, and his heart opened. The ordinary world he left behind had transformed into a tapestry of insights, rich experiences, and newfound understanding.

Now, with his adventure nearing its conclusion, Alexander stood ready to return home, carrying the weight of wisdom and the promise of change. The journey had shaped him into a leader, an innovator, and a harbinger of transformation. As he looked back at the footprints he had left on NexGen Island, he couldn't help but feel a sense of gratitude for the life-altering expedition.

And as the sun dipped beneath the horizon, casting a warm glow over the island, Alexander knew that the most profound change was yet to come. He was prepared to share the NexGen mindsets with his community, igniting a chain reaction of growth and innovation that would forever alter the course of their lives.

***

As Alexander's boat docked back at the familiar harbor, his heart pounded with anticipation and excitement. He had come a long way since he set sail, and he was eager to share his newfound knowledge and insights with his community. Stepping onto solid ground, he was greeted by familiar faces and warm embraces from friends and family who had eagerly awaited his return.

With a beaming smile, he walked through the streets of his town, taking in the sights he had missed during his absence. The buildings and houses stood just as he had left them, but everything felt different now. He noticed the intricate details of the architecture, the vibrant colors of the flowers in the town square, and the laughter of children playing in the park – it was as if his senses had been heightened by his experiences on NexGen Island.

As he approached the factory, he couldn't help but feel a mixture of nostalgia and excitement. The place that had once felt stifling and mundane now held the promise of transformation. He entered the factory, greeted by his colleagues with warm smiles and hearty handshakes. It was clear that they too were curious to hear about his journey.

Gathering them in the breakroom, Alexander began to share his experiences on NexGen Island. He spoke about the challenges he faced, the lessons he learned, and the profound impact it had on his perspective. As he narrated his encounters with the Sea of Lifelong Learning, the Forest of Human Behavior, and the River of Storytelling, his colleagues listened with bated breath, captivated by his stories.

"I've learned that growth is not just about acquiring knowledge or mastering new skills," Alexander emphasized, his voice filled with passion. "It's about embracing change, collaborating with others, and having the resilience to overcome failures. Each experience on NexGen Island has shown me the power of diversity and the importance of making an impact."

His colleagues nodded; their interest piqued by his words. They could sense the profound transformation in Alexander, and they were eager to learn from his journey. The factory, once a place defined by routine and monotony, was now buzzing with a renewed sense of purpose and curiosity.

Over the following days and weeks, Alexander continued to share his insights with his community. He conducted workshops on emotional intelligence, encouraged the use of modern tools and technologies, and fostered a culture of collaboration and innovation within the factory.

Alexander stood before a gathering of community members; their eyes fixed on him with eager anticipation. The factory's breakroom was now too small to accommodate the growing crowd, reflecting the widespread interest in hearing about his adventures on NexGen Island. With a deep breath, he began to recount his remarkable journey.

"As I sailed towards NexGen Island, I was filled with excitement and fear. It was a journey into the unknown, but I knew I had to embark on it to uncover the secrets that lay ahead," Alexander began, his voice steady yet brimming with emotion.

He vividly described the treacherous Sea of Lifelong Learning, where he realized the importance of continuous knowledge acquisition and the desire to learn. He recounted the challenges he faced in the Forest of Human Behavior, and how Sage's guidance on emotional intelligence helped him find his way.

His storytelling skills shone as he narrated his encounter with the Mountains of Modern Tools, where he harnessed the transformative power of modern technologies. The valley of Collaboration and Innovation had taught him the value of working together with diverse skillsets, and the River of Storytelling had revealed the power of narratives in connecting and inspiring.

"When I faced the Winds of Adaptability, I learned the significance of adjusting my sails to navigate change. And at the Garden of Diversity, I witnessed the strength that diversity brings to any team or community," Alexander continued, each word resonating with those who listened.

The crowd was captivated, hanging on to his every word, as if they were experiencing his journey alongside him. As Alexander shared his experiences, he could see the impact his stories were having on the community. Their minds were opening up to new possibilities, and the thirst for knowledge and growth was palpable.

"Through all these experiences, the most profound lesson came from the Volcano of Failure," Alexander confessed, his voice softening with sincerity. "I learned that failure is not the end; it's a steppingstone towards growth. Each eruption taught me resilience, and the importance of trying again, even when things seem impossible."

He saw nods of understanding from his audience, knowing that they had experienced their fair share of failures and setbacks in their lives. Alexander's vulnerability and honesty in sharing his own journey resonated deeply with them.

"As I stand here before you today, I can say with certainty that my journey on NexGen Island has transformed me. It has shown me that growth is not a destination but a continuous journey of self-discovery and improvement. I want to share these insights with all of you, to ignite a spark of change within our community," Alexander declared, his voice filled with determination.

The room erupted in applause, a testament to the impact of Alexander's words. He knew that his journey had not only transformed him but had the potential to transform his entire community as well.

***

In the weeks that followed Alexander's return, the community underwent a remarkable transformation. It started with small changes – individuals attending workshops on emotional intelligence, signing up for lifelong learning courses, and embracing collaboration in their everyday tasks. But these small steps soon snowballed into a collective shift in mindset that swept through the entire community.

The factory, once a place of routine and monotony, was now buzzing with creativity and innovation. Employees eagerly shared ideas and collaborated on projects, recognizing that their diverse skillsets and perspectives could lead to groundbreaking solutions.

Alexander's stories of adaptability during his encounter with the Winds of Adaptability inspired the workforce to embrace change fearlessly. They learned to adjust their sails and navigate through challenges, turning obstacles into opportunities for growth.

The once-frequent murmurs of skepticism and resistance to new ideas were replaced with an atmosphere of curiosity and open-mindedness. The community realized that failure was not a source of shame but a steppingstone to success. They were no longer afraid to take risks and try new approaches, knowing that growth came from embracing setbacks as part of the learning process.

In the heart of the community, a NexGen Learning Center emerged, offering continuous education and training to all members. The center became a hub of knowledge and innovation, fostering an environment of constant curiosity and exploration.

The impact of Alexander's journey on NexGen Island went beyond the walls of the factory. As the community members began to apply the ten crucial mindsets he brought back, they saw the world around them through a new lens. They embraced diversity, not just in their workplace but also in their interactions with the broader society.

Neighboring communities noticed the positive changes and became curious about the transformation. They sought guidance and collaboration from Alexander's community, recognizing the power of embracing change and cultivating a growth-oriented mindset.

The town's atmosphere shifted as well. People began to come together more often, organizing community events and initiatives. They celebrated each other's successes and offered support during challenging times, creating a strong network of mutual aid and encouragement.

***

As the months passed, the community's newfound resilience and innovative spirit began to draw attention from beyond the island. Researchers, entrepreneurs, and scholars flocked to witness the change firsthand, eager to study the community's transformation and learn from its success.

In this evolving community, Alexander found a renewed sense of purpose. He reveled in the joy of witnessing the positive impact his journey had on those around him. He knew that his time on NexGen Island had not only transformed him but had sparked a ripple effect of change that reached far beyond his own experiences.

The thriving society that blossomed from Alexander's journey on NexGen Island was a testament to the power of transformation and growth. In the factory, innovative projects were in full swing, driven by a newfound passion for continuous learning. Employees freely exchanged ideas, embracing the power of collaboration and diverse perspectives.

Emotional intelligence had become a cornerstone of daily interactions. Empathy and understanding flowed freely, fostering a supportive and inclusive environment. The community members appreciated the strength that came from diversity, celebrating the uniqueness of each individual and recognizing the potential that stemmed from varied backgrounds.

Resilience echoed through the streets of the town, as people faced challenges with determination and optimism. They no longer feared failure, but instead, they viewed it as a stepping stone to success. Mistakes were embraced as opportunities for growth and learning, and each setback was met with renewed determination to overcome.

The NexGen Learning Center stood tall, its doors open to all who sought knowledge and self-improvement. Lifelong learning had become a way of life, and the hunger for knowledge was insatiable. Workshops, seminars, and collaborative projects fueled the pursuit of excellence.

Outside the factory walls, the town had transformed into a vibrant hub of community engagement. People took pride in their shared accomplishments, knowing that they were part of a movement that was greater than themselves. Community events were frequent and lively, showcasing the power of unity and mutual support.

Neighbors from surrounding towns marveled at the changes they witnessed. The ripples of Alexander's journey had spread far and wide, inspiring others to embrace change and growth in their own lives. The once-stagnant community had evolved into a beacon of progress and hope, drawing visitors from afar to learn from its success.

***

With the town thriving and the community embracing the NexGen mindsets, Alexander couldn't help but feel a sense of accomplishment. However, there was one last thing he needed to do – seek out Sage. He had been eager to share the success of the transformation and to express his gratitude to the wise mentor who had set him on this extraordinary path.

As he walked to the place where he had first met Sage, he couldn't shake the feeling of excitement mixed with a tinge of sadness. When he arrived, he noticed the familiar compass lying on the ground. He picked it up and held it in his hands, taking a moment to reflect on his journey.

"Alexander," a voice whispered in the wind, and he looked around, but no one was there. "Sage?" he called out, hoping for a sign of her presence.

The wind carried her voice again, "Alexander, my dear, I'm here in your heart and in the spirit of this place. You have grown beyond what you could imagine, and I am immensely proud of you."

Tears welled up in his eyes as he realized that Sage had been guiding him all along, not in an actual physical sense, but in the wisdom she had instilled in him. She had become a part of his being, and her teachings lived on in the thriving society he had helped create.

With a mixture of sadness and gratitude, Alexander made his way to sit on the factory roof, looking out towards the horizon. The sun was setting, casting a warm glow over the transformed town. He felt a deep sense of satisfaction and hope for the future of his community.

"Sage, thank you for everything," he whispered to the wind. "Your wisdom will forever guide me, and I will continue to build upon the foundation you helped me lay."

As the stars began to twinkle in the night sky, Alexander knew that his journey was far from over. He had become a symbol of change and transformation for his community, and he embraced his role with humility and determination.

From that day forward, Alexander carried the spirit of NexGen Island with him, reminding himself and others to never stop growing, learning, and embracing change. The story of Alexander's journey spread far and wide, inspiring countless others to embark on their own quests for transformation and growth.

✳✳✳

And so, the legend of Alexander and NexGen Island lived on, not just as a tale of adventure, but as a reminder that the power of change lies within everyone – waiting to be unlocked by a desire for something more, something greater, something extraordinary.

As Alexander gazed at the stars, he knew that his journey was not just a tale of personal growth, but a testament to the power of embracing change and adopting a NexGen mindset. The community he once knew had evolved into a thriving, innovative society, united by a shared vision and fueled by the desire for progress.

In the distance, he heard laughter and joyful chatter, the echoes of a community that had embraced diversity, resilience, and collaboration. Each footstep on the path of impact had left an indelible mark, igniting a chain reaction of positive change that rippled through the town and beyond.

Alexander's heart swelled with pride as he realized that he was no longer just a dreamer yearning for change. He had become the catalyst, the spark that ignited the flame of transformation in the hearts of his fellow townspeople. Together, they had turned a once-static community into a beacon of hope and progress.

As the first light of dawn painted the horizon, Alexander knew that this was just the beginning. The adventure of NexGen Island had ignited a fire within him, a hunger to explore new horizons and create a world where dreams could become reality.

With a deep sense of purpose and gratitude, Alexander took one last look at the compass that had guided him on this extraordinary journey. He knew that its true power wasn't in pointing directions on a map, but in leading him towards a life of continuous growth and positive impact.

And so, with his heart filled with determination and hope, Alexander embraced the dawn of a new day. As he descended from the factory roof, he felt a profound sense of gratitude for the lessons learned and the transformation achieved.

The town that had once seemed ordinary now thrived with the extraordinary, and Alexander knew that he would forever be connected to the spirit of NexGen Island and the wisdom of Sage.

As he walked through the bustling streets, he couldn't help but smile, knowing that his journey was just one chapter in the ever-unfolding epic fable of life. The world was vast and filled with endless possibilities, and Alexander was eager to embrace every adventure that lay ahead.

As for the he NexGen mindsets live on, they live on, inspiring generations to come. As the story passed from one storyteller to another, it carried with it the essence of change, growth, and the power of a single individual to transform the world around them.

In the end, it wasn't just about the destination but the journey itself – the journey of self-discovery, of impact, and of becoming the hero of one's own story.

And thus, Alexander's tale becomes a timeless reminder that within every ordinary person lies the potential to embark on an extraordinary journey, leaving footprints of change and hope, forever etched in the hearts, minds, and spirits of those who dare to dream, to believe, and to embark on the adventure of a lifetime—personal growth, collaboration, and leadership.

Mindsets

BrainPower Bytes

Mindset 1: Continuous learning and personal growth

In the shifting sands of time, those who stay static are left behind. The mindset of continuous learning and personal growth is a critical cornerstone of success in any realm of life. It fuels the engine of improvement, powers the drive towards excellence, and shines the light of enlightenment on the dark corners of ignorance. It helps individuals adapt to the ever-changing landscape of life, evolve with the times, and turn challenges into opportunities.

However, those who lack this mindset may encounter various problems. They may stagnate, marooned on the island of yesterday, disconnected from the flow of the new. Their skills may become obsolete, their knowledge outdated, their perspective myopic. They may become complacent, content with the status quo, and resistant to change, oblivious to the shifting currents of life. Without continuous learning, they can lose their competitive edge, and without personal growth, they can become stuck in a rut, unable to achieve their full potential.

Developing this mindset starts with embracing change, not as an enemy, but as a friend. It involves being open to new ideas, hungry for new knowledge, and keen to step out of the comfort zone. Reading widely, engaging in diverse experiences, pursuing new hobbies, and embracing challenges are all practices that can aid in developing this mindset.

Furthermore, making learning a regular habit, like reading daily or taking up new courses, can help. Adopting a growth mindset, viewing failures as opportunities to learn, and celebrating small improvements also play a crucial role. Setting personal goals for growth, seeking feedback, and engaging in self-reflection can further catalyze the development of this mindset.

To apply this mindset, one can start by setting a learning goal each week, whether it's reading a new book, learning a new skill, or taking a new course. Creating a learning plan, tracking progress, and celebrating achievements can make the journey more enjoyable and rewarding.

In essence, adopting the mindset of continuous learning and personal growth is like planting a tree of knowledge in the garden of the mind. With regular nurturing, the tree can grow, its roots can deepen, and its branches can spread, bearing the fruits of wisdom, competence, and success.

Mindset 2: Constantly improving leadership skills

L eadership is not a static state; it's an ongoing journey of growth and development. Being a leader means being a guide, a beacon, and a role model. It means shouldering responsibilities, making difficult decisions, and inspiring others to do their best. But being a leader also means understanding that there's always room for improvement. The mindset of constantly improving leadership skills is what separates good leaders from great ones.

However, leaders who do not subscribe to this mindset might face numerous obstacles. They could fall into complacency, falsely believing they have reached the pinnacle of leadership. Such leaders might become resistant to feedback, viewing it as a threat rather than an opportunity for growth. This could lead to a decline in their leadership effectiveness, and consequently, a decrease in team performance and morale.

Developing this mindset is a matter of understanding that leadership is a skill, and like any skill, it can be honed and improved. This involves acknowledging one's areas of weakness, seeking constructive criticism, and being open to new ideas and approaches. Leaders can take courses, attend workshops, and seek mentorship to constantly enhance their skills.

To apply this mindset, leaders can start by conducting a self-assessment or seeking feedback from their teams about their leadership style. This can help identify areas for improvement. They can then create an action plan to address these areas, setting specific, measurable, achievable, relevant, and time-bound (SMART) goals.

Leaders can also dedicate time to learning about leadership theories and models, and incorporating these learnings into their own practices. They can seek mentorship from more experienced leaders and learn from their experiences and insights.

In sum, the mindset of constantly improving leadership skills is like polishing a diamond. With each round of polishing, the diamond's brilliance increases, and so does the leader's effectiveness. This not only enhances their own leadership journey but also positively impacts their team and organization.

Mindset 3: Understanding human behaviors and emotions in leadership

Leadership goes beyond strategic planning and execution; it delves into the heart of human interactions and relationships. Leaders who understand human behaviors and emotions are better equipped to motivate their teams, resolve conflicts, and foster a positive work environment. This mindset is at the heart of emotional intelligence – the ability to identify, understand, and manage one's own emotions and the emotions of others.

However, leaders who overlook the importance of this mindset might encounter several challenges. They could struggle with fostering meaningful connections with their team members. They might fail to understand the motivations, aspirations, and concerns of their team, leading to miscommunication and misalignment. Moreover, they might be unable to effectively manage emotional dynamics within the team, leading to unresolved conflicts, decreased morale, and lower productivity.

Developing this mindset requires a commitment to increasing one's emotional intelligence. This involves self-awareness, self-management, social awareness, and relationship management. Leaders need to reflect on their emotions and reactions, understand their triggers, and learn to manage their emotional responses. They also need to tune into the emotions of others, empathize with their perspectives, and effectively navigate social interactions.

To apply this mindset, leaders can start by taking the time to understand their emotions. They can journal about their emotional reactions to different situations, analyze their triggers, and devise strategies to manage their responses. They can also seek feedback from others about their emotional responses and impact on others.

Leaders can also enhance their understanding of others' emotions. They can observe verbal and non-verbal cues, ask open-ended questions to understand others' perspectives, and validate others' emotions. Moreover, they can seek training in emotional intelligence to further enhance their understanding of human behaviors and emotions.

By understanding human behaviors and emotions, leaders can foster stronger connections with their team members, enhance their leadership effectiveness, and contribute to a more harmonious and productive work environment.

Mindset 4: Leveraging AI and neuroscience to enhance performance

We live in a world where technology is reshaping the way we live and work. Artificial Intelligence (AI) and neuroscience offer powerful tools for leaders who seek to enhance their team's performance and drive innovation. Leaders with this mindset are open to embracing these advancements, continuously learning about these fields, and applying their insights to improve their leadership.

However, leaders who fail to adopt this mindset may face various challenges. Without leveraging AI, they may miss opportunities to automate mundane tasks, analyze large datasets for insights, or predict future trends, all of which can boost performance. Neglecting neuroscience's contribution can mean missing out on insights about human behavior, decision-making, and learning that can enhance team dynamics, productivity, and overall well-being.

To cultivate this mindset, leaders need to stay abreast of developments in AI and neuroscience. They can read relevant books, attend webinars or workshops, or even enroll in related courses. Leaders should also seek to practically apply their learnings. For example, they could implement AI-powered tools to streamline workflows or apply neuroscience-based techniques to improve learning and decision-making within their teams.

Further, leaders can create a culture that values these fields. They can encourage team members to learn about AI and neuroscience and provide resources for their education. They can also promote the use of AI tools and neuroscience insights in daily work, creating an environment that values innovation and evidence-based strategies.

By leveraging AI and neuroscience, leaders can optimize their team's performance, drive innovation, and stay ahead in the rapidly changing business landscape. The intersection of technology, science, and human understanding holds vast potential for those willing to explore it. Embracing this mindset can place leaders at the forefront of these exciting developments, equipping them to guide their teams towards a future shaped by knowledge, innovation, and understanding.

Mindset 5: Fostering a culture of collaboration and innovation for exponential growth

Innovation doesn't exist in a vacuum. It thrives in environments where ideas are freely shared, diverse perspectives are valued, and people feel empowered to experiment. Collaboration is the lifeblood of such environments. Leaders who understand this seek to foster a culture where collaboration and innovation are the norms, recognizing that this is key for exponential growth.

However, leaders who fail to cultivate this mindset can run into a variety of roadblocks. Without a culture of collaboration, silos can develop within the organization, leading to miscommunication, missed opportunities, and inefficiencies. Without fostering innovation, organizations may stagnate, falling behind in a rapidly evolving business landscape.

To develop this mindset, leaders can start by modeling collaborative and innovative behavior themselves. This means openly sharing ideas, valuing input from others, and demonstrating a willingness to take calculated risks. Leaders can also explicitly communicate the importance of collaboration and innovation, setting clear expectations for team behavior.

Moreover, leaders can create structures and processes that facilitate collaboration and innovation. This might involve creating cross-functional teams to break down silos, implementing platforms that enable idea-sharing, or setting up regular brainstorming sessions. Leaders could also recognize and reward collaborative and innovative behavior, reinforcing the culture they wish to create.

Finally, leaders must ensure that everyone feels safe to share ideas and make mistakes. This means fostering psychological safety, an environment where people feel secure taking risks without fear of punishment or ridicule.

When leaders foster a culture of collaboration and innovation, they set the stage for exponential growth. They create an environment where new ideas emerge, problems are solved more efficiently, and individuals feel more engaged in their work. This mindset is the bedrock of thriving, innovative organizations that are ready to tackle the challenges of the future.

Mindset 6: Overcoming traditional organizational dysfunctions

Organizational dysfunctions can significantly impede a team's performance and stifle innovation. These dysfunctions may manifest in many forms, such as a lack of trust, fear of conflict, avoidance of accountability, and a disregard for results. Without addressing these issues, leaders may find their organizations struggling with low productivity, high turnover, and poor morale.

Leaders who neglect to address these dysfunctions might find their organizations underperforming and their team members disengaged. This may lead to a toxic work culture, high employee turnover, and reduced efficiency, ultimately affecting the organization's bottom line. Moreover, unresolved dysfunctions may eventually damage the organization's reputation, making it difficult to attract and retain high-performing individuals.

To develop this mindset, leaders need to identify and acknowledge existing dysfunctions within their teams. This involves creating an environment where team members feel comfortable voicing their concerns and ideas for improvement. Leaders can also use team-building exercises, one-on-one meetings, and open forums to encourage communication and build trust within the team.

Next, leaders need to address the identified dysfunctions head-on. This could involve implementing new policies, providing additional training, or adjusting team dynamics. It may also involve difficult decisions, such as parting ways with individuals who are contributing to the dysfunction.

Finally, leaders need to continuously monitor their team dynamics and address any emerging dysfunctions promptly. By doing so, they ensure that their teams remain effective and their organizational culture stays healthy in the long term.

By overcoming traditional organizational dysfunctions, leaders can foster a work culture where team members are motivated, engaged, and productive. This not only leads to better results but also helps attract and retain talent, ensuring the organization's long-term success.

Mindset 7: The Power of Storytelling in Leadership

The ability to weave a compelling narrative is a potent tool for any leader. It can spark inspiration, create connections, and motivate action. However, leaders who underestimate the power of storytelling might face challenges in engaging their teams, communicating effectively, and influencing others.

Without the use of storytelling, leaders may struggle to keep their teams engaged. A well-told story can inspire, motivate, and align a team around a common goal, creating a sense of purpose and camaraderie. On the other hand, a lack of engaging narratives can result in a disinterested and disengaged team.

In terms of communication, storytelling can simplify complex ideas, making them more understandable and relatable. However, leaders who fail to incorporate storytelling in their communication might struggle to effectively convey their vision, leading to misunderstanding and misalignment within the team.

Furthermore, storytelling can serve as a powerful influencing tool. It can shape perceptions, drive behavior change, and inspire action. Leaders who don't leverage storytelling might find their influence weakened, impacting their ability to drive their team towards achieving their goals.

To cultivate this mindset, leaders can begin by recognizing the value of storytelling. This involves understanding its power to engage, simplify, and inspire. Next, leaders can hone their storytelling skills. They can study great storytellers, practice their narrative-building skills, and solicit feedback to improve.

In addition, leaders can incorporate storytelling into their daily interactions. They can use narratives to explain their vision, demonstrate core values, or highlight the importance of specific goals. By consistently using storytelling, leaders can inspire their teams, create a strong sense of purpose, and drive significant change within their organization.

A leader who masters the art of storytelling can inspire their team, effectively communicate their vision, and drive meaningful change. By leveraging this powerful tool, they can enhance their leadership effectiveness and create a strong, engaged team.

Mindset 8: Adaptability and Resilience in Leadership

L eaders in the modern world must be prepared for constant change. Whether it's technological advancements, shifts in the market, or changes within the organization itself, being adaptable and resilient in the face of these shifts is a crucial leadership quality. Leaders who lack these traits may find themselves ineffective during times of change, susceptible to stress and burnout, and underperforming in challenging times.

Ineffective leadership during change is a common problem for those who lack adaptability. When unexpected changes occur, these leaders may struggle to adjust their strategies or may resist the change altogether. This resistance can lead to missed opportunities, low morale within the team, and an overall decrease in effectiveness.

Lack of resilience can also lead to higher levels of stress and burnout. Leaders are often faced with high-pressure situations and challenging decisions. Those who lack resilience may become quickly overwhelmed and stressed, which can lead to burnout. This not only affects the leader's wellbeing, but it can also have a negative impact on their performance and their team's morale.

Additionally, leaders who lack adaptability and resilience may underperform during challenging times. They might struggle to find effective solutions to problems, become easily discouraged by setbacks, and may be unable to motivate their team during difficult periods.

To develop these qualities, leaders can begin by fostering a growth mindset. They should view challenges as opportunities for learning and growth, rather than as insurmountable obstacles. They can also practice flexibility in their decision-making, remaining open to new ideas and willing to change course when necessary.

Building resilience can also involve self-care practices, such as maintaining a healthy work-life balance, finding effective stress-management techniques, and seeking support when needed. By building these qualities, leaders can navigate through change more effectively, maintain their wellbeing under pressure, and lead their team through challenges to emerge stronger and more capable.

Mindset 9: Importance of Diversity and Inclusion in Fostering Creativity and Innovation

The inclusion of diverse perspectives, backgrounds, and experiences can significantly enhance the creative and innovative potential of any team or organization. Leaders who do not prioritize diversity and inclusion may find themselves working within teams with limited perspectives, poor dynamics, and potential damage to their reputation.

A team with homogenous perspectives often finds itself trapped in an echo chamber, regurgitating the same ideas and solutions. This lack of diversity can limit creativity and innovation, as fresh ideas, unique perspectives, and unconventional solutions are scarce. It's akin to looking at a multi-faceted problem through a single lens, which undoubtedly results in a narrow and potentially ineffective approach.

Without an inclusive environment, even the most diverse teams can encounter roadblocks. If team members feel undervalued, misunderstood, or sidelined, the dynamics within the team can sour. An inclusive leader not only recognizes but celebrates the individual differences within their team, fostering an environment where everyone feels heard, respected, and valued.

Organizations that do not prioritize diversity and inclusion may also face reputational damage. In today's socially conscious environment, an organization's stance on diversity and inclusion can significantly impact its public image. An organization known for its homogeneity and lack of inclusivity may struggle to attract and retain top talent, secure partnerships, and win customer loyalty.

Leaders can promote diversity and inclusion by fostering an open and accepting culture, actively seeking diverse talent, providing equal opportunities, and implementing inclusive policies. They can also invest in diversity and inclusion training and encourage diverse viewpoints during decision-making processes.

By embracing diversity and inclusion, leaders can tap into a wealth of ideas, foster a harmonious and productive team environment, and steer their organization towards a future of sustained innovation and success.

Mindset 10: Creating a Positive Impact in the Organization and on a Larger Societal Level

L eaders who do not prioritize creating a positive impact may face an array of challenges, including a lack of purpose, low employee engagement, and a potential blow to their reputation.

Without a clearly defined purpose that extends beyond profit-making, work may start to feel meaningless for both the leader and the team. A purpose-driven organization, however, can inspire its members to be more productive, innovative, and committed to their roles. This sense of purpose can act as a strong motivator, leading to increased job satisfaction and performance.

In the modern workforce, employees increasingly seek more from their employers than just a paycheck. They want to be part of an organization that makes a positive impact on society. If an organization fails to demonstrate its commitment to a broader purpose, it may suffer from low employee engagement and high turnover rates.

In the public eye, an organization's reputation is often linked to the impact it has on society. Organizations that do not actively strive to make a positive difference may face criticism and a potential loss of trust from their customers, employees, and other stakeholders. On the other hand, organizations known for their positive impact can enjoy enhanced reputation, customer loyalty, and the ability to attract and retain top talent.

Leaders can cultivate this mindset by setting a clear and meaningful vision for their organization, one that extends beyond just financial gain. They can communicate this vision to their team and integrate it into the organization's strategy and daily operations. They can also encourage and reward socially responsible behaviors and take a stand on important societal issues. By doing so, they can inspire their team to work towards creating a positive impact and drive their organization towards long-term success.

Afterword

As we come to the end of Alexander's transformative journey and the tale of NexGen Island, I want to take a moment to reflect on the lessons we've learned and the profound impact they can have on our lives.

We saw Alexander's development throughout the narrative from a young person desiring change in his unchanging community to a seasoned leader, armed with the ten essential mindsets he discovered on NexGen Island. His journey reminds us that embracing change and lifelong learning can lead to remarkable transformations.

After Alexander's return, he became a beacon of inspiration in his community. His newfound wisdom and courage helped him lead by example, guiding others on the path to growth and collaboration.

As Alexander shared his discoveries and experiences, we saw his community listen with bated breath, eager to absorb the knowledge that had brought about such positive change. It taught us the power of sharing our insights and how they can ignite a spark of transformation in others.

The most significant change we witnessed was in the community's mindset. By applying Alexander's lessons, they unlocked a wealth of possibilities and fostered a culture of innovation and collaboration.

The once-stagnant neighborhood had transformed into a thriving society thanks to the conviction that each person's individual strengths could aid in its development.

In the quiet moments of reflection, Alexander realized that his journey was not only about physical challenges but also about discovering his true self. He understood that the mentorship of Sage, though ethereal, had been a guiding force throughout his adventure.

As we conclude this epic fable, let us remember the powerful message it holds: Each one of us possesses the capacity to make a difference. The mindsets of NexGen Island are not fictional concepts but tangible tools that can elevate us in both our personal and professional lives.

Dear readers, the journey may end here, but your adventure is just beginning. As you close this chapter, let the spirit of Alexander's tale linger in your hearts. Embrace change, foster growth, and believe in your potential to create a lasting impact on the world around you.

May you embark on your own journey of transformation, fueled by the desire to learn, collaborate, and innovate. Remember that every step you take can leave footprints of change, shaping the course of your life and the lives of those around you.

And so, with a hopeful heart, I leave you with this thought: The NexGen mindsets are not limited to the pages of this fable; they reside within each of you, waiting to be unleashed.

Go forth and be the Alexanders of your communities, the leaders of innovation, and the guardians of progress. Let the legacy of NexGen live on in the impact you create.

Yours in growth, collaboration, and leadership,

Stephen Kincaid

About the Author

Stephen C. Kincaid is a seasoned Director of Product and Program Management at J.B. Hunt, a technology-oriented, industry-leading transportation and logistics company. His professional prowess, combined with a relentless pursuit of knowledge, has led him on a unique journey from the corporate halls to the world of literature.

Stephen's interest in neuroleadership and development extends beyond his role at J.B. Hunt. As the author of the popular "BrainPower Bytes," he provides weekly insights into strategic leadership and professional development, drawing from his rich experiences and ongoing studies. His writings have become an indispensable guide for many aspiring and established leaders looking to navigate their way through the ever-evolving corporate world.

Simultaneously, Stephen has a creative side that shines through in his charming and engaging children's books. These beautifully illustrated stories have not only brought joy to young readers but have also imparted valuable life lessons, demonstrating his ability to communicate complex ideas in a simple, enjoyable manner.

Stephen's educational journey reflects his dedication to continuous learning and his desire to contribute positively to the world around him. After earning his undergraduate degree from Hendrix College, he went on to pursue a Master's in Leadership from John Brown University, enhancing his understanding of organizational dynamics and effective leadership. He is currently pursuing a Doctorate at Liberty University in Instructional Design and Technology, a testament to his fascination with the intersection of education and technology.

Stephen's approach to writing, like his approach to leadership, is rooted in a firm belief in the transformative power of lifelong learning. He continues to explore the confluence of strategic neuroleadership, technology, and education, both in his professional career and his literary endeavors.

Whether he is writing an insightful piece on leadership or crafting a captivating children's tale, Stephen C. Kincaid brings a unique blend of expertise, creativity, and passion to every project he undertakes. His works are a reflection of his commitment to learning, growth, and the belief that everyone has the potential to be a leader in their own right.